HOW I OVERCAME GRIEF

HOW I OVERCAME GRIEF

How to Ease the Pain
Excerpts From Real Experiences

BY

Katherine Jones

ISBN 1-58500-465-0 (Paperback)
ISBN: 1-4033-7761-8 (Hardcover)

Library of Congress Control Number: 2002095426

This book is printed on acid free paper.

Printed in the United States of America
Bloomington, IN

1stBooks – Rev. 06/20/03

ABOUT THE BOOK

HOW I OVERCAME GRIEF is a self-help book for those struggling to get through the pain of grief. HOW I OVERCAME GRIEF is a collection of stories about people going through the grieving process. A lot has to do with ones upbringing. Every death experience is different, and everyone grieves differently; however, a decision not to grieve carries serious consequences. Powerful and explosive emotions are displayed when dealing with death, guilt, and anger and must be resolved. This book reaches out to people and tries to help them get a handle on their emotions, and impress upon them how importance it is to stay physically fit and mentally balanced. Grieving is a slow process and the results come a little at a time. HOW I OVERCAME GRIEF is thought provoking, positive, informative and uplifting. It offers hints, alternatives, and gives hope. The book is practical, down to earth, and easy to read and understand.

CONTENTS

Chapter 1 Grief 1
Chapter 2 Unresolved Grief 3
Chapter 3 Grieving the Dying of Another 9
Chapter 4 Mental Relaxation 13
Chapter 5 Grieving the Death of Another 15
Chapter 6 Scott Grieves Dying of Self 19
Chapter 7 Death of Scott 27
Chapter 8 My Buddy 33
Chapter 9 Secondary Losses and Unfinished Business ... 35
Chapter 10 Resignation 41
Chapter 11 Letting Go 45
Chapter 12 Grief, Sadism. and Masochism 47
Chapter 13 Grieving and Staying Well 51
Chapter 14 Grief and Emotions 55
Chapter 15 Physical Well-Being 57
Chapter 16 Social Adjustment 59
Chapter 17 Financial Grief 63
Chapter 18 Displaced Grief 67
Chapter 19 A Child's Grief 69
Chapter 20 Other Griefs 73
Chapter 21 Depression 75
Chapter 22 Anger 79
Chapter 23 Displaced Anger 81
Chapter 24 Guilt 85
Chapter 25 Suicide 89
Chapter 26 Reaching Closure 93
Chapter 27 Closure 95
Bibliography 97

CHAPTER 1

<u>Grief</u>

Adjusting to a loss is a slow endeaver, because you have to modify your behavior and change your attitude. Nobody likes change. Death is change, and change is necessary if you want to work through the psychological transistion which will enable you to disconnect and transfer the emotional energy you have invested in your love one into other persons, places, or things. Even when you believe death is "God's will," the grieving process is still vital.

Grieving is working your way through denial, anger, depression, bargaining, acceptance and closure. If you have never gone through a death of someone close to you, you're in for an unusual experience. Not having a "known," means you have nothing in your subconscious to desensitize or buffer the mental suffering.

Denial is the first step you take when dealing with death. Denial will keep you from believing what you know is true, but can't accept, and in an effort to bring the deceased back, he/she may become a figment of your imagination. The shadows you see here and the apparations you see there will only precipitate stress, disappointment, and more anger.

Sooner or later, you will have to accept the death. It has changed your life, and has either dashed or altered your future plans, dreams, hopes, and wishes. Death has suppressed your personality, and has taken away your positiveness and happy-go-lucky disposition. Death has turned your outlook on life negative and fatalistic. Your belief system has been damaged and you must seek to repair and rebuild your emotional foundation.

Grieving has a way of waking you in the middle of the night and making you wonder what can possibly happen to you next. You must take care that the pain which comes with grieving doesn't sap your energy and leave you limp, lethargic, and panicky trying to make sense out of death. Your coping mechanism will force you, in time, to adapt to the concept of death.

CHAPTER 2

Unresolved Grief

This is the result of failing to let go and find closure. Unresolved grief comes from the agony and pain precipitated when you're forced into a separation. Nothing hurts more than being deprived of someone you love. Death throws you into a quandary of misery, anger, mental, physical, and emotional turmoil. You hurt because of the loss. You're angry because you've been deprived, and to find relief you must go through a grieving process to adjust to the agony, and resolve the anger.

For many people, the hardest part of grieving is letting go and accepting the finality of death. There's no doubt death hurts. It's painful to disconnect and change the emotional relationship you had with the deceased. But it's even harder to dissipate or transfer the emotional energy you had invested in the deceased into another person, place, or thing. Separating is painful, but necessary, if you ever want to reach some form of closure.

Not going through a grieving process, whatever the reason, will come back to haunt you. You can't just bury your grief. You can run away from it, but you can't hide from it. It will come back. The unresolved emotional trauma will flare up when you least expect it in the form of deviant behavior. Failure to go through a grieving process only prolongs the inevitable.

Situation: Calvin was eleven when he lost his grandmother. They were on their way home after a fine dinner with Pastor King and his wife. Calvin's mother, Shiela and stepfather Ralph, were chatting away in the front seat. Calvin was sitting with his grandmother in the back. The sun was setting, and all of the car windows were down. The conversation was jovial and everyone was enjoying the cool late spring air blowing against their cheeks. Ralph pulled up to a four-way stop sign in their 1938 Ford sedan. He looked, and when he saw it was clear, he proceeded to cross the intersection. Half-way through, a 1940

Studebaker came roaring down the road doing around seventy mph. It didn't stop. It plowed through the intersection broadsiding their car.

Their car flipped over rolling four times before stopping. Calvin was knocked unconscious, and when he came to, two men were pulling him out of the wreckage. He was facing down. When he opened his eyes and saw his grandmother, she was dead. Her head was partially crushed and one blue eye was open and staring at him. He was so traumatized that the moment the men laid him down on the ground, he freaked out. Calvin got up and started running across a freshly plowed field. The two men that pulled him out took off after him, and tackled him to the ground a half mile away. Each took an arm and marched him back to the restaurant across the street from the accident scene, and sat holding him on a chair.

Calvin's parents came in, and sat across from him to wait for the ambulance to come pick up his grandmother's body. All he heard were people telling his parents how sorry they were and hugging them. What about him? Not one person was paying him any attention. Nobody concerned themselves that he might be hurting. He sat quietly feeling alone and abandoned. He was shivering and worried about what was going to happen to him-his grandmother had been his whole life. He couldn't imagine living without her. She had raised him, and what would he do. He never bonded with his mother and wasn't close to his stepfather. The hollow empty feeling in his stomach, and the need for closeness made him vomit.

At this time in Calvin's life he needed love, guidance, and support. He needed something tangible to hang on to and feel secure, but there was no one to console him, sympathize with him, or hug him. There was no one to tell him everything would be all right. Being ignored and left to suffer alone was the beginning of his feelings of rage. Did it matter that Calvin had been hit in the head and knocked out? No! Did it matter he had a gash in the back of his head. No! The doctor said he was okay and that made everything all right. He was sent home with his parents, and when he became dizzy a couple of hours later, he didn't say anything to his parents. He excused himself and went to bed. He dealt with the pain in his head and the pain in his heart by himself.

Calvin cried himself to sleep. By morning, the headache was gone, but the pain in his heart remained. He didn't know how to deal with grief, and knew nothing about the stages. He didn't even have a "known" in his subconscious to relate to. All he had was a premonition that he was in trouble.

At the inquest he attracted attention when he sat alone staring at the woman who killed his grandmother and brought so much pain into his heart. When he heard someone comment on how hard he was looking at the lady, he got up and went outside. At that moment he hated her for being drunk, and if looks could've killed, she'd be dead. She had deprived him of love, compassion, guidance and understanding. She had thrust into his life pain and suffering he didn't know how to deal with.

After the funeral, Calvin went through all the motions of appearing normal, going to school and all, but he couldn't concentrate. He was depressed and began escaping into day dreams. His grades dropped, and he rebelled. He definitely needed counseling to help him get through the tragedy. He needed someone to show him how to grieve and how to cope with the agony of death. His mother wasn't supportive because she had her own problems.

Calvin had no positive role models or friends he could go to, and nobody to replace his grandmother. Until he reached high school, he was all but ignored and left to fend on his own, but when he got into high school sports and made a name for himself, everyone wanted to be his friend.

Calvin dropped out of college because of adjustment problems, and enlisted into the navy. He volunteered for combat and survived because of his sadistic/masochistic attitude. In hind sight, Calvin wishes the navy doctors helping him with his stress, would've used some of their psychology to help him work through his personal as well as his wartime grief because when he was discharged, he walked out of the navy carrying more psychological baggage than when he entered.

Half the people in our society walk around daily in a state of anxiety because too much input from the environment, physical body, conscious and subconscious mind, is being sent to the brain. They are "overloaded", because they're fearful, deprived, depressed, angry, stressed or grieving. In this condition, people do irrational things. Their conscious mind has shut down allowing incoming message units to flow in uncensored, directly into the subconscious mind. That's dangerous because that mind has no intelligence and doesn't know right from wrong.

The conscious mind is only 12% of your life's script, and it handles your will-power, logic, reasoning, objectivity and decision making. The subconscious mind deals with feelings, emotions, the imagination, and handles 88% of your life script. The subconscious mind doesn't think, use logic or reason, that's why it is so important when a person is involved in death and dying they go through a grieving process.

Death stresses people out, and makes them mentally and emotionaly unstable. That's why Calvin took off running when his grandmother was killed. He was using his primitive fight/flight mechanism trying to escape. Later in life, and still having no closure on his grandmother's death and wartime experiences, Calvin's psychological problems began to show themselves in male aggressions turned outward. In addition, he developed skin problems. He took delight in inflicting physical and psychological pain on others. He was sadistic and "got off" on hurting people. It made him feel superior. Calvin was adept at attacking one's personality and brutally cutting them down. His skin problems worsened. He became a chronic hand washer, and suffered from allergies.

Situation 2: Eva lost her father when she was four and his death left her permanently damaged. Her unresolved grief and anger came out in phobias. Eva was the fifth of six children, and didn't get adequate nurturing from her mother after her father died.

Effect: Eva turned her unresolved grief and anger inward and her problems exhibited themselves in the form of "cleanness". She couldn't tolerate stains, specks or spots on sheets, or the covers she slept under. If Eva found something in her bed, be it night or day, she'd get the purex bottle, make hot soapy suds, and proceed to wash the soiled area. Once the stain was washed out, she'd plug in the iron, lay a towel over the wet area and steam it dry. She'd become frantic if the speck didn't come out and would strip the bed and wash everything. Food was also a problem. Being forced to eat something she considered unclean was thrown-up.

Eva's mother never had to worry about her wanting to eat or sleep overnight with friends, and when the family visited relatives, Eva checked the beds thoroughly. Before getting into any strange bed, she'd dress in pajamas. She resembled an Eskimo with nothing exposed except her hands and face. Covering her skin gave her some kind of psychological security that kept her from developing a "nervous itch". Wrapping up allowed Eva to relax, get the mental images out of her mind, and sleep most of the night without having nightmares about what she had seen on the bedding.

Growing up on the farm without adequate explanations added to Eva's clean phobia. She saw too much too young and formed unhealthy opinions when watching farm animals mate, give birth, and suckle their young. Procreation became repulsive and the act of sex nasty. Watching mothers in church nursing their babies reminded her of the very animals she saw in the barnyard.

Eva didn't realize what losing her father really meant until she was in high school and started thinking about her future. Without her father, her life chances were severely limited, and that brought on rage that lowered her resistence. She contracted valley fever and spent a year in a sanitarium. Her dad was a good provider and would've had the means to help her realize her dream, but instead, she had to settle for second best.

Even though she was angry, once out of the sanitarium, she found a live-in job, worked her way through business school and became a secretary. Eva never felt fulfilled. She never got over feeling angry and cheated. Eva had a great life physically, but personally she never accomplished anything that made her feel her life was worthwhile. This feeling sometimes depressed her.

CHAPTER 3

<u>Grieving the Dying of Another</u>

Situation 1: Sabrina grieved the dying of her son, Josh, before he expired. Josh was at war and wearing a bulletproof vest when he was cut down in a hail of bullets from a rival gang. He went into the hospital in critical condition under an alias where he lay between life and death for days while police kept gang hitmen at bay.

When Sabrina visited her son, she was terrified and numb with fear. Her heart pounded in her ears as she looked at her first born hooked up to machines with tubes everywhere. She was paranoid, and feared retaliation.

She and her son were close and the gang lords knew that. Fearing for her life, Sabrina made a habit of looking over her shoulder when she left home, and at night she slept with a loaded gun under her pillow. She was in a heightened state of anxiety and didn't know from one minute to the next what was going to happen. While fearing the worst, she began going through the stages of grief. Josh's dangerous life style enabled her to skirt through denial and replace her anger with fear.

When Josh was ambushed and killed during the second attempt, Sabrina felt relief. This time she was prepared. She had developed a "known" in her subconscious that allowed her to identify with her son's pending demise. When he was buried, Sabrina had no more expectancy. Her son was definitely gone, and she could seek closure.

Usually with gang killings, parents appear to skip from denial to acceptance because of their child's lifestyle. They know the inevitable is just a matter of time, and they grieve in advance. When death occurs, if there is any anger, it's probably due to being deprived of their child, but if the child does not die and ends up paralyzed or mentally damaged, and he/she becomes a financial burden, there lies the real anger. Parents feel that they didn't ask for this burden. When a gang member is killed, the mentality of those left behind is to retaliate. Closure to them comes in the form of getting even. Their actions are akin to the New Guinea Tribes in the South Pacific. When they catch the perpetrator who killed one of their family members, he is cooked and served as an entree for the victims families and relatives.

Situation 2: When Scott noticed his dad and wife had been crying, he wanted to know why. And as soon as they left the room, he turned to his mother and asked what exactly did the doctor say about his condition. Frieda looked at Scott and folded her arms. A pained expression covered her face as she looked across the room. Having to tell her son he was going to die was the hardest thing she'd ever have to do.

She took a deep breath and said, "Scott, your health doesn't look good. There are lots of things wrong the doctors can't fix, and your doctor doesn't think he can save you. We're losing the fight and there's nothing we can do, son."

Scott stared at his mother in disbelief, then said, "Mom, I don't want to die."

"I know son, and I don't want you to die," Frieda said staying calm and concealing her rage.

That was the moment Frieda denounced God and medicine. That was the moment it became crystal clear there was no damn God, and if there was, he or it wasn't worth a damn. All of her praying had been a waste of time, and it was at that moment, Frieda abandoned the concept of God and everything religion was supposed to stand for.

Scott must have read his mother's thoughts, because he put his hand on her arm and said. "Don't worry, Mom, we've all gotta go sometime. I've had a good life. I've lived in the fast lane, driven fast cars, traveled all over, ate in the best restaurants, and accomplished everything I set out to do. My only regret is not seeing my young son grow up.

I believe what you taught me, that when I leave this world I will simply enter into another dimension of living. Life is like a circle with no beginning and no ending. Mom, I'm not frightened. Dad taught me to take my medicine like a man, and if this is it, so be it."

Two months later Scott's health worsened and he moved

home so his parents could care for him. One morning when Frieda looked in on Scott, she noticed something was wrong. Scott looked odd. He had a vacant stare that frightened her. Frieda called Mario. He checked his son, and figured he had been restless during the night, had gotten up and taken a couple morphine pills to put him to sleep. Even though they kept pills hidden from Scott, they knew he had a supply stashed somewhere for emergency use.

At nine, Scott wanted to go to the bathroom and called his dad to assist him. He asked his mother to fix his breakfast, but when she brought a tray of food, he couldn't eat. Scott's coordination was off--he kept missing his mouth and his parents took turns feeding him. When he finished, he drank a glass of water with a straw then laid back on his pillow. Mario made Scott comfortable, then left him to sleep-off the effects of whatever he had taken.

Scott slept for three hours, and when he awakened, he got out of bed and walked downstairs where his worried parents were. "Hello," he said on his way to the refrigerator to get something to eat. Scott helped himself to a handfull of grapes, then sat down. He told his mother he was starving, and asked her to fixed him a big plate of food while he and dad talked.

The first thing Mario wanted to know was if Scott remembered what had happened earlier. He said he didn't have a clue and shook his head "no". Mario dropped the subject.

The next morning, Mario and Frieda purposely got up early to observe Scott. Nothing seemed out of the ordinary. He awakened at eight, got out of bed and went to the bathroom like normal. Mario helped him in and out of the shower. He dressed himself, then went to the kitchen to watch cartoons until breakfast was served.

The next few weeks, Scott's health improved along with his appetite, and he began putting on weight. He was excited, and the saying, "if it ain't broke don't fix it should've prevailed, but didn't. Scott was a gambler and wanted more. When he went for his medical check up, not only was he looking good, he was feeling good. He begged his doctor to give him a diet to help him keep putting on weight and he did without considering the consequences. He gave Scott a high carbo diet.

Mario and Frieda were furious because Scott was non-compliant when it came to eating. They were concerned about the yeast and stomach cramps that were under control, but in a terminal case, Doctor Stone was only concerned about making his patient happy. And he did. Scott was excited, and on the way home, he asked his dad to stop so he could buy an ice cream sundae. He was so starved for what he considered "good food," he went hog wild.

At home, the first thing Scott wanted was lasagne, salad and garlic bread.   And that week, he ate like a pig and drank everything in sight except liquor.   He got his fill of whole milk, condensed milk, shakes, and fruit juices.

Scott ate cottage cheese, cream cheese, regular cheeses, sugar, sour cream, pies, bakery goods, eclairs, wheat breads, and candies. He and Sherri went out for soul food, Chinese, Mexican, and Italian dinners. Eating whatever he wanted was the happiest Scott had been since leaving his job to go on disability. He rationalized about all the foods he was eating and figured, "what the heck ... you only live once."

CHAPTER 4

<u>Mental Relaxation</u>

Without meditating and practicing deep relaxation, Mario and Frieda wouldn't have made it through the trying period of grieving the dying of their son. Deep relaxation calmed their bodies, relaxed their minds, and gave them the strength to continue on.

Find a comfortable place. Lay back, legs apart, with arms at your side. Prop your head up.

Step 1
1. Stare at a fixed object.
2. Breathe deeply three times.
3. Pick one of the following words: relaxation, lightness, floating, tingling, comfortable, heavy, or warm.
4. Concentrate on that word.
5. Place your hands on your thighs.
6. Close your eyes and breathe deeply three times.
   Concentrate on the palms of your hands.
   Allow relaxation to flow from your feet to your lower legs, thighs, shoulders, and on to the top of your head. Then go back down to your feet. Do this three times.

Step 2
1. Pick a word from this group: happy, calm, confident, successful, peaceful, positive, or pleasant.
2. Concentrate on that word.
3. Breathe in deeply and exhale slowly three times.

Step 3
1. Turn your attention to your eyes.
2. Concentrate, and say DEEP SLEEP six times.

Step 4
1. Read, or memorize this suggestion and give it to yourself verbally: "Forgiveness and love are a part of the deep universal feeling inside me. I am relaxed, in control of my life, and have a shield around me that keeps out all negative ideas, thoughts, suggestions, and inferences from everyone and everything."
2. Now say, "each and every time I suggest DEEP SLEEP, I will go quickly, soundly, and deeply asleep."
3. Do this suggestion three times.

Step 5
1. At the end of your session, count yourself out.
2. Say... 1-2-3-4-5 ... Eyes Open...Wide Awake.
3. Repeat the above three times.

The mental anguish and suffering that accompanies the death of a love one is the most devastating crisis you will ever face in a lifetime. Use self-hypnosis, it will give you the strength and self-confidence needed to move you through the grieving process without getting bogged down in anger, self-pity, stress or frustration.

Listen to high self-esteem subliminal music. Turn it on a half hour each morning before you get out of bed. The positive music and messages will energize you, lift your spirits, and help you start your day off feeling up-lifted. Later in the day, practice deep relaxation, stare into a fish aquarium, or listen to sounds of the ocean splashing water and birds cooing in the distance. These are helpful tools to calm you.

CHAPTER 5

<u>Grieving the Death of Another</u>

Situation 1: Anna doesn't believe she ever grieved for her mother. She thinks she spent too many years grieving for her when she was addicted to prescription drugs and was psychotic. Anna lived everyday thinking her mother would die any moment because of her lifestyle. She became hardened and unemotional about death as it related to her.

The night Anna learned of her mother's death, she didn't cry. She just accepted it because she knew it was inevitable. She turned out the light and went to sleep. She cried at her mother's funeral because she felt it was expected of her. People were watching and what would they say if they didn't see a public display of grief. As a matter-of-fact, she recalls it was her cousin sitting next to her, who encouraged her to cry. So, she did. Anna said to herself. "If I don't cry what kind of message will I be sending to my own child. Will my daughter think it's not right to cry at your own mother's funeral?"

Anna was so detached and disconnected, she felt no pain then, doesn't feel any now, and doubts she ever will. She thinks her mom's death made her more aware of how precious time is, and she wants to spend what time she has left being the best mother and wife she can. She wants her daughter to grow-up with happy memories of her childhood and her relationship with her mother.

Anna was sad she wasn't able to have a normal relationship with her mother before she was diagnosed with cancer. When Anna received the news, she knew she and her mother didn't have much time to learn to be friends. She felt she couldn't be her friend or assist her during her illness until she could discuss with her, her abnormal behavior during her childhood. She wanted to know why her mother routinely abused her physically, and she didn't want her to depart from this earth without being told how she personally felt about what went on in their home when she was growing up.

Anna forced her mother to talk to her about her childhood. She knew it was difficult, but talking enabled them to create a better, more mature, and friendlier relationship than what they previously had. Her mother admitted she used prescription drugs and abused her family, but she never apologized. Anna realized her mother's denial was a display of her mental illness. She forgave her, but will never forget how difficult it was living with her as a parent. Anna believes her mother tried very hard to be a better mother and friend as she approached the end.

When her mother expired, Anna felt like a chapter in her life had ended and she could move on. She didn't feel angry that her mother was gone, and she didn't feel guilty that she was not at her side when she expired.

Anna spent the last five days of her mother's life nursing her. She didn't want her to die alone in the hospital, and would have never returned to her home and family had she known her sister, who agreed to come and relieve her, couldn't make it. All of the sisters were notified the day Anna checked their mother into the hospital. They all knew she was dying and had ample time to come, help out, and say good-bye.

Had Anna avoided her mother during her illness, and hadn't helped when she needed assistance, she thinks she would've felt a sense of guilt and shame. She knows she did her very best to assist her parent, and her mother appreciated it. They both experienced a bond that hadn't previously existed, and her mother knew she sincerely wanted to be with her, provide comfort, and companionship regardless of what had happened in the past. Anna thinks she has this attitude because she has also been critically ill and near death.

Any person who has gone through a death experience, will be able to bypass some of the mental conflict that goes along with death because of conditioning. They will have developed a "known" in their subconscious that can associate, identify, and relate to the pain connected with death. However, if you have not gone through a death experience, you won't have a "known" to buffer some of the pain. You will go through pure hell, and suffer an ungodly amount of mental, and physical anguish.

Death and dying will throw people into a hypersuggestible state. This state will make you tired and you'll seek escape through sleep. Sleep is the best relief for grief. It's an escape mechanism. Use it, and use time as an ally. Time softens the pangs of death. Use it to help you adjust, take control of your emotions, and work to bring order and balance back into your life.

Situation 2: Rhonda was almost pain free when her mother expired. She had experienced most of her pain at the end of her mother's life when there were so many physical demands placed on her. Rhonda needed extra strength and energy to do things for her mother, take care of her husband, and give support to her daddy, family members, and friends. She wasn't angry when her mother died, and believed she was truly blessed because her death was easy. Her mother was able to be at home with her family almost to the end, and was spared the (tubes in every orifice), ritual of a hospital death.

When Rhonda needed to cry, there seemed to be triggers to her tears everywhere, and she'd cry and cry. Rhonda found it easier to enjoy these releases when she was alone and didn't have to explain anything to anybody. There were times, she was profoundly saddened by not having her mother and cried because she felt alone. Then she'd retrace memories of her mother, reminiscence, and find enough good things to bring joy back into her life and lightness in her soul.

The day Rhonda's mother expired, she had visited with her family, and that night she went to sleep and never awakened. That was merciful. Rhonda doesn't know if her family shares that belief, but she thinks her mom's response to her illness and her realization of its finality, helped her get through her death without any feelings of guilt.

Her mother never complained. There were no "why me's," and she found joy in the small things her children could do for her. She enjoyed it when they cooked her favorite meal, helped her with her personal care, and be there for her when they could.

CHAPTER 6

<u>Scott Grieves Dying of Self</u>

Death never fightened Scott, it fascinated him. He believed he was moving into the next sphere of existence, and dying was like completing the circle. "From Him I came and to Him I will return." He had a cult-like mentality and Mario purposely steered him clear of involvement with other people who were curious about dying. Scott believed in kismet, "what will be will be," and whatever happens in life is fate, pure and simple be it good or bad.

When Scott was sick, he often asked questions about what dying was like. He speculated and fantasized about where the trip would take him. He believed there was a supreme logic to everything, but if there was a God or a place called heaven or hell he needed more proof. But once Scott realized he would never get well, he was anxious to "get it on," any place was better than staying on earth grappling with his disease.

Mario put Scott in the driver's seat. He told him he was the captain of his ship and the master of his soul, and when he was ready, he could go anywhere he wanted, just close his eyes and float off into the blue just like they had talked about.

Scott called the shots all the way. He was determined he had to live past April '92 to secure his family's financial future, but definitely wanted to be gone by Father's day.

Frieda will never forget June 9th when she came home from work. She thumbed through the mail, then went to check on Scott. He was sitting up in bed waiting for her with a pencil and pad in hand.

"Hi, Mom," Scott said gleefully. "Get a pencil and paper and sit down, I've got something to tell you, and you're not going to like hearing what I'm going to say. But please understand."

Frieda figured Scott wanted to talk about his will or Tony's education. No way, was she prepared for what he had to say as she pulled up a chair, kicked off her shoes and sat eagerly waiting.

"Mom, I'm ready to die. I'm tired of living. I'm tired of being sick, tired of hurting, tired of the food I've got to eat, tired of the way I look, and tired of the way I feel. I'm tired of having to take so many pills, tired of going to doctors, tired of their lies, and in short, I'm just tired of being tired ... period! I know I'll never get well, and I want you to understand why I want to die. I would've gone today, but I didn't want to frighten you when you came home. I know how sensitive you are about living in houses where people have died, and I respect your feelings."

Frieda's stomach started swirling as the force of Scott's words sank in. Not knowing what to do or say, she sat dumbfounded with mouth open and eyes wide. Sensing his mother's anxiety, Scott paused for her to gain her composure.

"I know how you feel, mom. Don't cry. Just write down my requests, and please comply.

Cook me some good food before I check out. As long as I have to die, I want to go with a full belly and a taste of good food in my mouth. Fix me a chocolate cake with chocolate icing, buy me a hot fudge sundae, and some of those delicious chocolate candies I like," Scott said.

Then he took a sip of water, sat back and began complaining about how disgusted he was with his eye, his yellow body and losing the cap off his tooth. He was unhappy he couldn't gain more weight and felt his body was falling apart and shriveling up. Scott reminisced a few minutes about growing up, then got out of bed to go to the bathroom. When he returned, he thanked Frieda for being a good listener, and for everything she and dad had done for him in health and in sickness. He was happy they gave him a good start in life and he had the foresight to follow through and earn a college degree, and make the three things he wanted most in life come true. He landed a job in management, got married, and had the baby he always wanted.

Scott desperately wanted his mother to understand his situation, respect his wishes and let him go. He had been a good son, had given her many good years, and was leaving behind a grandson to take his place.

"Mom I know it's going to be tough, but if it makes coping with my loss any easier, pretend Tony is me and move on. All good things eventually comes to an end, and I strongly feel it's time for me to hang it up and for you to let go, I've been a burden long enough. You and dad need to get out and travel, and when you do, hang one on for me. It's time for me to get on with where I'm going, I've imposed long enough," Scott said looking seriously at his mother.

Scott told Frieda he had no regrets. He didn't want to die, but when he looked back over his life, he was able to fulfull his dreams and accomplish everything he set out to do. Then he smiled and said. "Mom, I've lived a good life. I just hate not seeing my child grow up."

"Wow!" Frieda said standing up. "Let's go to the kitchen, and you tell me what you intend to do about Sherri and Tony. You still have a lot to live for even though you're sick. Tony needs his father for guidance. We're living in very precipitous times."

Scott nodded his head in agreement, took a deep breath and smiled slightly. He put his hand on his mother's, looked into her eyes and said. "Mom, stop trying to put a guilt trip on me. Sherri and Tony will survive, and my dying will be doing them a favor. This isn't me! When I look in the mirror I don't see me. I see somebody else looking back, and if what I see and feel is any indication of the quality of life I'll have if I live, I don't want it. Let me go. You have dad, Sherri has Tony, Frank has Virginia and not letting me go is selfish."

"I've been working with Sherri, and have gone over survival skills. I've shown her how to handle finances, reconcile the checkbook, and she knows what bills to pay-off. I've urged her to refinance our home, and to put your mind at ease, I've written a guideline for her to follow should she run into any problems. She'll be fine. She has always wanted a diamond ring and I told her to buy herself one. Take a trip, don't let anybody cheat her out of her money, and take care of our son. If she screws up it will be her fault," Scott said.

"I've asked Frank to be a big brother to Tony, and be the role model I can't, and teach him discipline and values. I want everybody to instill good character qualities into Tony, and show him how to handle male aggression, channel anger, and what being a male is all about," Scott said.

"I've given Frank and Virginia my blessings, and Mom," Scott said smiling, "I've told Frank I'll come back and kick his butt if he calls off his wedding. If I don't make it physically, I'll be with him spiritually. I'll be standing beside him cheering him on. I like Virginia. She's a nice lady and will do right by my brother."

Suddenly, a thought struck Scott. He sat up in his chair, looked at Frieda and said, "Mom would you mind if I died in my room close to you and Dad?"

"I certainly do," Frieda said looking startled. "You came home to get well, remember? Dying wasn't part of the agreement. Now, if dying is your aim, consider a hospice."

Scott looked hurt for a moment, then smiled and said. "I was just joking. I wouldn't do that to you, and I won't come back after I've gone."

"Scott, we've always been close. Stop worrying about dying, we'll cross that bridge when we get to it," Frieda said.

"You're right," Scott said picking up his written notes. "Let's get back to my departure."

Scott didn't want Sherri spending a lot of money on an expensive funeral, and asked his mother to get some burial information. He wanted to be laid out in the cheapest casket because everybody had spent enough. He wanted his casket closed with a picture of him and one spray of flowers on top.

Scott was sensitive, and wanted family and friends to remember him when he was robust, in good health, and looking good. He thought one limousine would be enough to carry the family to and from the cemetery and saw no need to waste money hiring uniformed escorts to direct traffic. That would be an unnecessary expense. He didn't want it, and Sherri didn't need it.

Scott wanted to keep the funeral small, costs down, and the ceremony short. He asked his mom to dispense with those stale, tear-jerking, old-time religious songs and play his favorite, "Take Me Home".

Scott was jovial and made Frieda smile when he talked about not wanting a lot of crying, screaming and howling over him.

He didn't want Sherri overcome by emotions and falling out on the floor acting undignified. Frieda patted Scott's hand and assured him everything would be just like he wanted.

"Good! With that settled, I can take care of me," Scott said.

Frieda went to the cupboard to get Scott's pills. "You will continue taking your medicine as prescribed, and eat?" Frieda asked. "You may have a change of mind."

Scott nodded. Frieda watched Scott stir the cup of chocolate she placed before him. He cooled it with cold water, then took his pills in two gulps. He finished his chocolate, put the cup in the sink and kissed his mother goodnight on the cheek and headed for bed.

Frieda sat at the table thinking, then laid her head down on the table and cried softly. Her head ached and her heart was heavy. After awhile, she got up to go to bed. Scott was snoring when she checked on him. She kissed him good night on the forehead and muttered. "I love you son." She turned out the light and went to her room.

The next morning, Scott was at the kitchen table waiting to pounce on his dad. Mario poured himself a steaming cup of coffee and sat across from Scott. When he finished doctoring it up with sugar and cream, he looked at his son and said, "What's up?"

"Dad, did mom tell you I'm ready to check out?"

"Yeah," Mario said.

"I need your help, first," Scott said. "I want to go after July."

"Scott, I can't help you. It's too risky. The archaic laws dealing with euthanasia won't allow me to do what you want. Helping you that way is illegal, and Sherri and Tony won't receive the money you want them to have. It's not easy to die when money is involved. You can't check into a hospice like a hotel, order a large quantity of morphine and sleep yourself to death. It just doesn't work that way," Mario explained.

Scott was disappointed, and sat staring at the floor. After what seemed like an ungodly long time, he looked at his dad, and for the first time noticed the suffering in his face.

"Dad, I'll try to hold on a little longer." Scott said "Maybe they'll find a cure."

"Are you guys okay?" Frieda asked coming into the kitchen.

"Everything is fine," Scott said. "Mom I want you to go shopping for me. I'm going to try one last time to put back on the weight I lost. I haven't had any luck following dad's diet, and since the doctor's diet nearly killed me, I want to try my diet."

Frieda slipped into a pair of shoes while Scott wrote out his grocery list. She wanted to get to the market before it became crowded. When Frieda returned, the guys came out and carried the bags of groceries inside. Mario and Frieda helped Scott put the food away, then turned the kitchen over to him. They went upstairs to watch television.

Scott washed, put on an apron and got busy chopping up veggies for one of his favorite Mexican entrees. The aroma coming from the kitchen was mouth-watering, and when he was ready to dine he called his parents to come join him. They did, but only ate salad.

The next morning, Scott was still on a high. He showered, dressed, and hurried into the kitchen. He was going to prepare himself a special omlette, a muffin, and a glass of juice. So far, so good, but by noon on the third day, the party was over. Sharp pains streaked through his gut. Mario gave him a small bit of morphine to ease the pain and practiced "laying on hands," (a holistic approach), but Scott's affliction was too powerful. By the end of the day, Mario took Scott to the hospital.

Some people when grieving dying-of-self, are bombarded with fears about their immortality. That comes from the repressed primitive memories tucked away in their subconscious. These survival instincts trigger the unthinking impulse of self-preservation that comes from genetic heritage, evolved learning, and conditioning. Other people when grieving dying-of-self are actually grieving pre-death fears: who will care for me, who will feed me, and support me physically and emotionally when I can no longer care for myself.

In Frieda's case when she grieved dying-of-self, she became horrified just thinking about being forced to eat food prepared by people she viewed as unclean, but in Scott's case, coming home solved all of his pre-death fears. He had emotional security, love, and support. His meals were prepared, pills counted and given on time. His dad was there to help him when he had difficulty moving around, and his mother offered positiveness and a bright outlook on life. His brother was a supportive companion all the way and Scott needed that.

When a person completes the dying-of-self stages: anger, denial, depression, bargaining, acceptance, and closure, all of their psychological baggage should be resolved.

All guilt and self-guilt should be overcome and replaced with self-forgiveness. Any fears about personal care during the years, months and days preceeding death, should be put to rest. If there are family or business problems, resolve them and tie up the loose ends. Take care of business so that toward the end you will be able to relax.

If there are such things as restless ghosts, I would think, they were the result of some people dying before they were able to complete the stages of dying-of-self which are: denial, anger, bargaining, and acceptance.

When going through the dying-of-self stages, put your mind at ease and resolve some of your "what if fears and phobias," by doing the following:

1. Set up a living trust and will.
2. Pick someone you trust to look after you, handle your business and personal affairs and be supportive and compassionate.

3. Join a senior citizen group for companionship and travel if you can.
4. Live in a retirement community where all of your needs are met and taken care of.

CHAPTER 7

Death of Scott

When Scott reminisced his past, present, and future, he had only one regret--not seeing his son grow up. His life had had meaning and his time spent on earth had been worthwhile. He had made a difference. He accepted death and felt immortalized. You can feel immortalized if you can fit into one of the following categories. Have you?

1. Achieved or created a worthwhile product that will live through the ages: i.e., an invention, a position that secures a place in history, being a part of a scientific break through, a philanthropist, an artist, musician, author, architecture, etc.
2. Developed a strong belief in a religion or an afterlife.
3. Replaced yourself through procreation.
4. Made a difference by developing a high sense of purpose for living.

Whether a person leaves this world quietly or dramatically, immortality is relevant. Bonnie and Clyde enjoys the same notoriety as statesmen, presidents or kings.

People think about many things when they are grieving death-of-self or death-of-others. Some try to visualize their demise, some secretly hope to come back, and others wonder about other dimensions. The light people see before becoming unconscious is when the brain stops receiving oxygen, and the imaginary things people say they see comes from floaters in their eyes.

Let's get back to Frieda. She awakened at six, looked at the clock, then slipped out of bed to go check on Scott. Mario waited for her to return. When Frieda entered Scott's room, he opened his eyes, smiled, and said. "Go back to bed. Mom, it's too early to eat. Fix me some Malt-o-meal about nine."

Frieda smiled and returned to bed. She told Mario he seemed all right, but she didn't know those were the last words she'd ever have with her son. Two hours later Scott called his dad to come help him walk to the bathroom.

Mario was leaning against the sink talking to Scott about last night's transfusion when Scott pitched forward. Mario caught him and sat him upright on the commode, but he kept falling forward.

"What's going on, Scott?" Mario asked in a panic.

He looked into his son's eyes and his heart sank. That all too familiar "stoned" stare was back. Mario's mind was in a quandry wondering what had happened, what was happening, and what would happen. Scott was fine a minute ago. Did the nurses give him something; had he taken an overdose of morphine? What was wrong?

Mario purposely removed his hands from Scott's shoulder and when he fell forward his last words were, "Oh dad!" Mario caught him and carried him back to bed hoping he would come out of whatever was wrong with him after a few hours of sleep. Frieda made him comfortable, tucked the blanket around his shoulders while Mario checked his pulse. Everything appeared normal.

At ten, Frieda brought breakfast and they tried to get Scott to sit up and eat, but he couldn't. He kept falling over, even when his dad propped him up with pillows. He wouldn't eat. He shook his head slightly and closed his eyes.

Frieda took the food back to the kitchen while Mario made Scott comfortable. When he joined her, they sat in a daze staring at each other.

At one o'clock, Mario decided not to go to work, his intuition was telling him to stay close. Since there was nothing Frieda could do, he encouraged her to go to work and she did. When she left, Mario stood in the hall for a long time listening for sounds. The house was deathly quiet except for the ticking clock and running water in the aquarium.

Not knowing what to do with himself, Mario decided to shave. He walked upstairs, checked on Scott, then went into the bathroom, but came out every five minutes to check on Scott. The third time, there was a definite change in his son's condition. His breathing was erratic and coming once every fifteen to twenty seconds. Realizing Scott was going into respiratory standstill, Mario administered mouth-to-mouth resuscitation. The moment Mario got Scott breathing more normal, he called 911, Sherri, and Frieda.

When Frieda arrived back home, Sherri and the paramedics were there. The first paramedic checked Scott and thought he was dead. The second thought he was diabetic and in insulin shock. Mario suggested they check his vital signs. They did, and immediately administered oxygen and started an I.V.

Two firemen came in, put Scott on a stretcher, and two others helped carry him downstairs. They loaded him into a waiting ambulance. Sherri thought she had been prepared for this horrible day. She couldn't believe her loving husband was leaving her. She wanted to reach out to him, but there was nothing she could do. She climbed into the ambulance and touched Scott's hand lightly. He didn't move and she wondered if he was in pain. Sherri talked to Scott all the way to the emergency facility. She wanted to cry, but tears wouldn't come.

The ambulance was gone when Mario jumped into his car and speeded to the hospital. He wanted to get there and advise the emergency room staff not to do cardiac compressions. Scott was too frail, and he feared they'd break his ribs. Scott's heart wasn't the problem, it was his respiratory system.

Frieda paged Frank, phoned Virginia and instructed both to meet them at the hospital emergency room.

Scott was still unconscious when Frank and Virginia arrived. They had him on life support and in I.C.U. where he would stay until his condition stabilized and he could be transported to hospice.

As soon as Sherri completed the admitting paper work, Mario left for work and Frieda went home to rest. Frank, Virginia, and Sherri stayed with Scott.

After Frieda had rested for an hour, she got up and began vacuuming and cleaning Scott's room. She didn't think he would be coming home, but if he did, she wanted his room to be fresh.

As soon as Frieda jerked the sheets off Scott's bed, loose pills and packages of pills flew everywhere.

"I'll be damned, the little stinker wasn't taking his medicine.

That's why he insisted on keeping his room clean himself," Frieda mumbled.

Frieda always respected his space and privacy and allowed him to make whatever decisions and choices he wanted. Apparently, hiding his pills and eating all the foods he enjoyed was one of his decisions. Loose pills were hidden under the bed, in drawers, in pockets of clothing, the waste paper basket, the hamper, and God only knows how many were flushed down the toilet or garbage disposal.

When Frieda finished her pill search, she sat on the bed wondering what other surprises were in Scott's room. She checked his suitcase, and found packages of cigarettes, containers of his special mouth wash, packages of candies, chocolate cupcakes, and cookies.

"He told me he was going to leave this world with a taste of good food in his mouth, and he wasn't lying," Frieda said, picking up the phone to call Mario. Mario wasn't surpised and told Frieda, Scott had been taking additional Prednisone to mask his pain so he could freely eat all the junk foods he wanted. When he ran out of the drug and abruptly stopped, he triggered a Prednisone dump that caused his blood sugar to drop to a level deleterious to life. Test revealed he had a blood sugar of ten when he checked into the emergency room.

"Do you think he knew what he was doing?" Frieda asked.

"He was no dummy," Mario replied.

That night the doctor on duty wanted to disconnect Scott's life support and let him go, but the family wasn't ready. The doctor felt keeping Scott alive was cruel, and would serve no useful purpose. He was too far gone. Mario called and explained to the doctor that the family wanted Scott to stay on life support until he stabilized and could be transferred to hospice. If he didn't stable out in two days, they'd give consent to have the life support removed, and if he couldn't breathe on his own, they'd let him go.

Sherri, Frank, and Virginia stayed with Scott all night, and with the help of oxygen, Scott was conscious, aware, and communicated with slight smiles, head movements, and blinks of his eyes. He couldn't talk due to tubes in his mouth and nose.

Sherri rubbed his brow while Frank and Virginia talked to him about sports, news, his son, and their up-and-coming wedding. When Scott slept, they slept.

The next morning Scott motioned to his brother to pull the plug, and it pained Frank not to comply knowing the pain he must have been in, but he had to be responsible and explained to his brother why he couldn't. Scott understood and nodded his head.

Virginia, Frank and Sherri left at ten when Mario and Frieda arrived. Mario went in alone to see Scott and make his peace. He felt guilty and had to explain to him why he brought him back to life--why he had broken a promise by rescusitating him.

Mario held Scott's hand and told him how sorry he was, and that he couldn't let him go without giving his wife, mother, brother, and son, an opportunity to tell him goodbye. He couldn't let him go into respiratory standstill. He had a responsibility to save his life, and a responsibility to his family.

Mario asked for Scott's forgiveness. Even though Scott was angry, he forgave his dad. He bowed his head and squeezed his dad's hand indicating forgiveness. Mario was relieved.

"Thank you son. Now, I'm putting you back in the driver's seat. Do you want the life support removed?" Mario asked.

Scott nodded his head yes. His dad told him as soon as he stabled out and could be transported to his hospital, all life support would come off, and in accordance with his wishes, there would be no code blues should he stop breathing. Scott agreed and a slight smile crossed his face. That's what he wanted.

Mario blinked back a tear. Having made peace with his son, he left the room with tears in his eyes. Frieda patted him on the shoulder, then went in to see her son. She talked to him about how much she'd miss him, how much she enjoyed having him as a son, and how much she loved him. When the nurse came in to check Scott and the equipment, he seemed tired. Frieda kissed him and promised to let him go.

Scott smiled slightly as his mother patted him on the forearm. She told him she'd visit him again in the evening and urged him to get some sleep because his in-laws would be spending the afternoon sitting with him.

It took two days before Scott was fully awake, conscious and breathing on his own. Life support was removed, and an ambulance was ordered to transport him to a skilled nursing facility.

The next day Scott slipped into a coma. Tony was brought in to tell his dad goodbye, and that night a chaplain was brought in to administer last rights, and pray with the family. Frank was with his brother talking sports, eating a burger, and watching television when he slipped away in the early morning of July 15th. Virginia stayed with Tony when the family gathered at Scott's bedside. They reminisced about Scott until the wee hours of the morning.

Finally, Mario said, "We'd better wrap it up and do like Scott suggested, let him go and get on with our lives. We'll all miss his smile, jokes and sense of humor."

Mario hugged everyone, then kissed his son goodbye. Frank walked over and kissed his brother. Frieda stood and gazed at her boy before walking over and leaning down. She stroked his forehead then whispered, "I love you Scott and will never forget you." She kissed him and quickly left the room. Sherri was the last to leave. She held her husband's hand and whispered goodbye, kissed him and walked away crying.

CHAPTER 8

<u>My Buddy</u>

Scottie and Mario symbolically grew-up together. Mario never had a brother, and his son Scott, gave him much of what he lost growing up. Scott was a friend, confidant, and partner. He was Mario's hero, and when he died a part of Mario died.

It was pure hell watching Scott grow feeble. He was losing his son and there wasn't a damn thing he could do. Helplessness is a terrible feeling. Although Mario had seen his share of death and dying and had "knowns" in his subconscious to desensitisize the pain, he still wasn't ready for Scott's death.

Every death Mario witnessed after Scott was gone, left him with a lump in his throat, a sick feeling in the pit of his stomach, and a heart that sometimes flipped inside his chest like a ping-pong ball. Mario was prepared for Scottie's physical death, but not for his spiritual loss. It has taken Mario years to reconcile and disconnect. The bond between them was strong.

Mario will always grieve Scott. He was the brother he never had. Mario was a role model and father. Scott made him feel like somebody. He made him feel important and worthwhile. He gave him something no other male had--a sense of maleness, and an identity. Scott respected Mario as a father, and was shown a caring and guidance Mario never had growing up. Scott undoubtedly related to his dad's neediness and reached out to him.

CHAPTER 9

<u>Secondary Losses and Unfinished Business</u>

Grieving the deceased is only part of the grieving process, there are secondary losses and unfinished business one must work through. The secondary losses are the unpleasant activities that went on between you and the deceased: the conflicts, disagreements, jealousies, likes and dislikes, habits, traits, personality quirks, clashes, mannerisms, and attitudes, etc. Any interaction that took place between you and the deceased that leaves you with feelings of remorse, anger, and guilt, must be grieved individually, and the best way to do that is through repetition.

Make a list of all the emotional interactions between you and the deceased that makes you feel sad or sorry. Say or write each vicious thing you did or said to that person, and repeat it over and over and over. If you need to apologize for something, write an apology or say it until you feel vendicated. Each time you remember something painful that happened, and let go of it, the pain becomes a little less, and you withdraw a little more of your emotional investment. Reviewing each painful incident brings you a little closer to putting closure on that emotion.

Secondary losses deals with the emotions, and unfinished business with tangible objects. When grieving unfinished business you may have to set aside your anger in order to make sound business or legal decisions that will effect your future well-being. Grieving unfinished business is therapeutic because you must get involved, learn all you can and then take control.

If your spouse left a company to run, had a lawsuit hanging, or some unfinished real estate venture in limbo, taking control and resolving each problem allows you to grieve and put closure on each item and the emotion drawing you to the deceased. Whether you're grieving secondary losses, or making decisions concerning unfinished business, every resolution makes you a little bit stronger and better able to cope and withdraw a little more of your emotional energy from the deceased.

When Harriet awakened to find Nathan motionless and cold, she was in shock. She shook him, but he didn't move. Realizing he was gone, she called 911, her children, then sat down and quietly looked at Nathan until paramedics arrived. They ascertained Nathan was dead and called his attending physician. He had seen Nathan just three days ago and agreed to sign the death certificate. With that information, they loaded Nathan into the ambulance and took him to the Northstar Mortuary.

Harriet felt a tinge of guilt. Did she contribute to his death? They had been arguing that night about doctors, their bills, and the poor care they were receiving. Nathan wanted to find another doctor, but she didn't want to change, and both were upset when they went to bed.

When the ambulance left, Harriet sat down to think about what to do next. They had been married fifty some years and now she was alone. Her world had caved in around her. She felt numb, detached, abandoned, and scared. She didn't want to live with her children, but she couldn't stay alone. Anger swept over her. She pounded the table and cried. "Nathan! You had no right to die and leave me ... without you I can't care for myself... I can't drive ... I'm in poor health ... what will I ever do?"

For whatever reason, Harriet never liked funerals. She was angry, depressed, and made no exception for Nathan. The children made all the arrangements, and in accordance with Nathan's wishes, funeral services were held to twenty minutes. Harriet didn't want to see Nathan laid out in a coffin.

After Nathan was buried, Harriet went to live with her children. She ignored all unfinished business and only agreed to rent the farm house. Everything else stayed in limbo. The land laid dormant, weeds grew, trees died, farm equipment rusted setting in the elements, and the tires on the automobiles decayed. Harriet wanted the farm to stay exactly the way it was when Nathan died. That was her last link to him, and she wasn't about to let go.

In Harriet's case, she would've been better off had she turned the task of unfinished business over to her son, he would've made responsible decisions concerning her future. Instead, she lost money on the farm. Her stubborn attitude strained relations with her family, prolonged her grieving,and stood in the way of her children putting closure on their dad's death.

In many cases grieving unfinished business is easier than grieving secondary losses because of the emotions involved. Harriet had become half a person. She had lost half of what she used to be. Her best friend and confidant was gone. She had no one to drink her morning coffee with, or cook a special dish for. She had no one to argue or joke with, or go on trips with. Her sex partner was gone and her social life had changed. Harriet's standard of living had been altered, but worst of all, she had no one to take care of her. Overnight she lost her independence, hopes, dreams and expectations. Nathan's dying left her dependent, frightened, worried and having to rely on her children which she resented.

Harriet had many secondary losses, and the first one she needed to resolve was to admit she was angry. Secondly, she needed to identify what she was angry about, and third, make a list of the losses she needed to grieve. Once she did that, she could begin asking herself various questions about her relationship with Nathan. Did she tell him goodbye. If not, that should be the next item on her grief list.

When Harriet finishes grieving her goodbyes, she should ask herself was their relationship a happy one? Was she happy? Were there any emotional needs and wants that were unmet at the time of Nathan's death? Does she have any regrets? Was he a good partner? Were they communicating effectively? How angry was she when she went to bed the night he expired?

Harriet should talk to Nathan directly about the dreams they had, the projects she needs to complete, and the plans they had that will never materialize. If she has difficulty talking out loud to Nathan about money, business, and legal matters, she should find a family member, friend, or minister to talk to. Write letters to her mate, or find ways to express her feelings. Become creative, learn to paint, sew, play the piano, grow a garden, etc.

If Harriet needs to tell Nathan how sorry she is he died, and how much she loves and misses him, all she needs to do is review the uncomfortable memories one at a time using repetition. The more Harriet reviews each feeling, the faster she will be able to dissolve the hurt. Once she's desensitized, it will become easier for her to withdraw her emotional energy from Nathan and transfer it into something constructive.

When Harriet has grieved all of the losses linking her to Nathan, she will be able to bring closure to the relationship and move on with her life in a healthful manner.

Read the following affirmation to help you facilitate and resolve problems surrounding death and dying.

> I am imagining a scene that relaxes me and makes me feel comfortable and focused. Although, I'm alone, I feel secure and confident. I know what I must do, and I must find a way to set the pains of death aside, focus, concentrate and remove the painful cloud hovering over my head and affecting my thoughts. I need strength to come out of my fog and begin making decisions. There are problems I must solve if I am to go on. Even when I don't think about my problems, my attention is drawn to the things I have to resolve. To resolve my problems, when I enter my office, I go into a relaxed state. And while looking through papers and documents, I allow solutions to enter my mind. Some catch me by surprise and others come to me in the wee hours of the morning when my mind is a clean slate. As I delve into the decision making process I am becoming stronger, steadier and less distracted. I am able to concentrate more easily, think more clearly, and arrive at sound solutions. My self-confidence is growing and fears of failure are disappearing. Each day when I enter my work place to make decisions, I am becoming more independent and have a greater personal feeling of security and safety with the decisions I make. I am learning to trust my own judgement and feel less need to rely on the

opinions of others. I'm finding that my final solutions are realistic, practical and right for all involved. Making decisions is therapeutic and makes me feel good about myself.

CHAPTER 10

<u>Resignation</u>

<u>Situation 1</u>: Death is change, but Dolly didn't feel the impact of the change until she stood at the foot of her sister's bed, and watched her slip into eternity. She knew she was happy to be wherever she was from the expression of peace on her face. A tear of joy rolled down the side of her face. At the funeral Dolly was calm, until the pall bearers put her sister's casket into the hearse at the church. She felt like screaming at the top of her voice. She was so overwhelmed her head felt like it was going to pop open. This was it. She knew it was all over for her to ever see her sister in the physical sense again. She would never again communicate with her because she was now in God's hands.

When they reached the cemetery and the casket was lowered into the ground, Dolly felt total relief. A burden had been lifted off her shoulders. Her sister would have no more physical pain and suffering, and she was free to go on with her life.

After the funeral, Dolly never shed another tear, but she still thinks of her sister and still misses her. However, as time goes by, missing her is like a passing thought. She smiles as she thinks about her, the times they enjoyed together, the trips they took, and the conversations they had.

<u>Situation 2:</u> Virginia experienced death at an early age. She was twelve when her mother died, and she thinks her religion and clergy packaged death so neatly, and explained it in such a way, her emotions were suppressed. All she felt was resignation. Years later, Virginia still isn't sure she knew how to grieve then or how to grieve now. As a child, she didn't know about the classic way to grieve: denial, anger, depression, bargaining, and acceptance.

She did a lot of talking to family, friends, and anyone who remembered her mother. Talking was therapeutic and enabled Virginia to accept the reality that her mother was really gone. Talking lessened her sense of loss and made her feel more at peace.

Virginia physically resembled her mother, and when looking at old photos or in the mirror, she was able to keep her mother's memory alive by looking at herself. People always knew whose kid she was when growing up, because she and her mother looked so much alike. Virginia was a joy to her mom when she lived. She did what was expected of her, and never gave her any grief.

Some family members were angry when her mother died, but not Virginia. Anger wasn't an emotion she could associate with her mom's death. She believed that if she were to be angry, she would be angry at God, and that wouldn't be fair or wise because good and bad happens simultaneously.

When Virginia feels upset, it mostly pertains to the realization that she can no longer hug and kiss her mother physically,and must resign herself to believe that she resides in a better place and they will meet when she dies and goes to heaven.

Be aware of the danger anger, resentment, and guilt can cause. These emotions will burn up energy unnecessarily, inhibit the healing process, and contribute to mental and physical turmoil. Read or write the following affirmation, and let it help you work toward acceptance and put closure on the deceased.

> There is a divine spirit that heals as it flows through me. When I call upon it, it relieves my pain, and helps me understand the meaning of death. Forgiveness and love are what universal power is made of. Going through the process of grieving, there is a divine spirit that helps me let go of inner tensions, and free my mind and body of anger, resentment, and guilt. Through focusing daily on love and forgiveness, I am able to identify who I need to forgive, and reach out to them. I fill the space occupying guilt and resentment with love, understanding, and forgiveness. With help from the ever present and powerful healing spirit, I am able to forgive

myself and forgive others. I am able to dissipate the feelings of anger, rage, and the resentment churning inside me. By allowing the spirit of forgiveness to grow within, I become more receptive to lifes' healing forces through love of God, and forgiveness of self and others.

CHAPTER 11

Letting Go

Now that you know grief is pain, anger, and mental turmoil all in one package, you can understand why you feel so bad, and why that empty never-ending feeling won't go away. The hurt associated with grieving is so powerful, it forces you to find ways to disconnect your emotional and physical energy and re-invest it into a substitute. The transfer is painful, but separation must come about if you are to accept the finality of death, and change the relationship you had with the deceased when he or she was alive.

When Frieda lost her son, Scott, she desperately needed a crutch to help ease her emotional pain, and for the next four years, her grandson replaced her son. His presence helped her through the maze of grief, and when she disconnected from her departed son, she was able to disconnect from her grandson and set him free. She was able to see him as an individual in his own right and not a replacement of her son. He was an extension of Scott, not a reincarnation.

Frieda created a symbol of her deceased son and established a ritual in his memory. She planted three beautiful rose bushes in the front yard. One white, one red, and one yellow. These were his favorite colors, and whenever she steps outside, she remembers her son.

Once a year, the family participates in a ritual to celebrate Scott's birthday, and keep his memory alive for his son, Tony. They burn candles, reminisce, look at old photo books, memorabilia, sing songs, and tell scary stories.

The following affirmation helped Frieda create happiness when she was able to change her thinking after a long bout with grief:

> Grieving makes me aware that when life's situations don't turn out the way I want, I must work to change the situation, or myself with as

little frustration, anger, and pain as possible. When grieving and working the things that are not the way I want, I can accept them with dignity, calmness and peace of mind. I'm learning to be resilient, and understand that when it comes to death, I'm not alone. As I grow and mature, I will face other obstacles with a clearer mind, and with more strength and determination. I am working to improve my situation, but if I find I cannot change my outlook for the better, I will always have an alternative, one that will enable me to better accept the outcome of my loss calmly and with confidence. Having a second solution will help me control the anger and frustration death has created. My life is too precious and too wonderful to fret over what I can or cannot control. I try to work to change what I can and accept what I can't change. All any of us have is "now". Yesterday is dead and gone, and tomorrow may never come. I work in the here and now, and will get through the grieving process and put meaning back into my life.

CHAPTER 12

<u>Grief, Sadism. and Masochism</u>

It's not politically correct to call attention to the sadistic and masochistic traits people exhibit when grieving. These traits are usually swept under the rug, and grieving people never know why they acted out the way they did. When a close love one dies, death often brings out the worst in us, and that includes the sadistic and masochist characteristics everyone has.

These two traits are like mood swings, and most of the time the individual doesn't know which one is the more dominant or in effect at any one time. Hostility is conscious, and hostile actions are expressed directly if the person is more sadistic. If the person is more masochistic, the hostility will be unconscious and the actions will be indirectly expressed.

Let's take the case of Calvin. When his grandmother was killed, he never grieved. He was too angry. He carried his unresolved anger and grief around for forty years before he went out of control. He was restless, and used being on the move and running as an escape mechanism, but when he hit age fifty, he could no longer maintain a balance between his sadistic and masochistic tendencies. Repressed memories and unresolved guilt and anger took over his personality. His behavior changed, and before he knew it, his darkside reared its ugly head and all of his past psychological baggage hit him like a ton of bricks.

Calvin never grieved his grandmother's death and never resolved his anger toward her for dying and leaving him at the mercy of his uncaring parents. To get rid of the rage he had been carrying around for years, he needed to find a look-alike woman he could hurt. Calvin had an overwhelming need to inflict pain. Inflicting pain made him feel good. The woman he needed to find would have masochistic tendencies. She would enjoy pain and allow him to get rid of his unresolved anger.

The woman he was searching for would be his look-a-like grandmother with blue eyes, blond hair and a hooked nose. Two years later he met such a woman by accident at an office party.

She was the perfect fit, and they clicked psychologically. This woman was raised in an abusive environment and had a "known." Calvin had witnessed men beating their women while growing up and he bad a "known." One was programmed to administer pain and the other to accept pain. She was a masochist accustomed to being hurt, and Calvin was a sadist programmed to hurt.

Beating this woman, inflicting psychological, physical and mental pain relieved the rage buried inside Calvin. He received satisfaction from beating, choking, and nearly drowning this woman in an effort to release and get the bottled up rage out of his system and bring his sadistic and masochistic characteristics into balance. Calvin played with this woman like a cat plays with a mouse before the kill, and luckily he came to his senses before he got around to killing her. Killing her would've been the ultimate high and would've put closure on the persons he hated the most--his grandmother and mother.

Calvin and this woman had a love-hate relationship. She loved him, but he hated her and used her. Both were mentally sick at the time, and this example goes to show just how dangerous and destructive unresolved grief and anger can be when allowed to fester for years.

Mild forms of grief and anger are expressed through acts of nervousness, having a short temper, being intolerant, belligerent, or just plain frustrated. Most of the time, mild forms of unresolved grief and anger are taken out on people close by, like family, friends, doctors and nurses. Mild forms of grief usually pass in a short period of time.

Medium forms of grief generally give way to exercising, running, ripping phone books apart, throwing dishes, chopping wood, pulling weeds, screaming, swearing or beating a pillow or boxing bag. These are excellent ways of working through grief and anger. They help keep your sadistic and/or masochist tendencies in check. Whenever anger begins to turn to rage and you find yourself losing control, watch out! You need grief or anger counseling stat. Get help. Don't become a danger to yourself and society.

Some people keep their masochist tendencies in check by flirting with death. They live on the edge. They channel their destructive energies into dangerous activities such as: racing cars, boats, or motorcycles, mountain climbing, stunt flying, etc. Others may get hooked on excessive drinking, gambling, womanizing, drugs, or fighting, etc.

Those who gamble and take their S&M drive to the limit often get drawn into criminal activities with the intent to hurt or be hurt. Commiting murder, robbery, drive by shootings, boxing, or having unprotected sex when HIV positive are a few examples.

It is believed that people with extreme S&M characteristics have suffered some form of unresolved trauma in their lives. Take for instance the two men shot by the police in the North Hollywood, California, bank robbery, or the man who robbed the same bank four times. They were sadistic and masochistic. They wanted to hurt and be hurt.

In view of the fact that S&M traits are part of everybody's personality, it's the degree that determines how much a person will deviate from what is considered normal behavior. Look at grieving as being a sickness. If you don't go through a grieving process to get well, and heal your emotions, attitude, and mental state, you will remain ill.

Until you reach acceptance and can disconnect and transfer your emotional energy to another person, place or thing, your psyche will remain unbalanced and the slightest stress will create a deviant attitude.

Think of grieving as a way to channel your morbid thoughts into avenues of positiveness and joy. Think of anger as the emotion that triggers the release of adrenalin that prepares the body to take flight or fight. And finally, think about how important it is to keep your personality balanced.

CHAPTER 13

<u>Grieving and Staying Well</u>

As you try to re-think your life as you grieve, remember your health. Every event that takes place in your life affects you. Each event demands a certain amount of change, and each change precipitates a certain amount of stress. Getting sick is the last thing you need if you're grieving. Enduring a death can be the most traumatic change you will ever go through, the closer the person, the greater the change.

Follow the preventive measures outlined and reduce your chances of becoming sick in the future:

A. Changes:

1. Familarize yourself with each life event and how much adjustment it requires?
2. Identify each feeling you experience with each event.
   Find ways to adjust to each event.
   Take time when making a decision.
   Try to anticipate a life change and prepare for it in advance.

B. While going through the grieving process:

1. Talk about the deceased with someone you trust.
2. Use the problem solving method:
   (a) recognize a change
   (b) determine how it will affect you
   (c) define what the change is
   (d) figure out the best way to handle the change
3. Draw from past experiences. Go with the tried and proven.
4. Set goals and make plans. Be flexible.
5. Always have an alternative.

C. Six basic items that will keep you healthy are: deep

relaxation, yoga, meditation, exercise, adequate sleep, and nutritious foods.

D.   Use the following test as a guideline:

Life Changes	Number Value
1. When husband or wife dies	200
2. Dissolution of marriage	173
3. Legal separation	165
4. Time in jail	163
5. Death of mother, father or sibling	163
6. Physical injury or sickness	153
7. Getting married	150
8. Terminated from job	147
9. Reconciling your marriage	145
10. Retiring	145
11. Family member's health changes	144
12. Having a baby	140
13. Sexual problems	139
14. Addition to the family	139
15. Readjusting your business	139
16. Financial status changes	138
17. A close friend dies	137
18. Career change	138
19. Fewer arguments with spouse	135
20. First mortgage exceeds $10,000	131
21. Facing foreclosure	130
22. Change in job duties	129
23. Children grow up and leave home	129
24. Feuding with in-laws	129
25. Extra ordinary personal accomplishment	128
26. Spouse starts or stops working	126
27. Start or stop school	126
28. Living conditions have changed	125

Life Changes	Number Values
29. Adjustment of personal habits	124

30. Problems with boss.. 123
31. Hours and work conditions are changed 120
32. Residence is different.. 120
33. School is different 120
34. Recreation is different 119
35. Church activities have changed............................ 119
36. Social activities have changed.............................. 118
37. Loan or mortgage below $10,000......................... 117
38. Sleeping habits have changed............................... 116
39. Number of family gatherings have changed......... 115
40. Eating habits have changed 115
41. Going on a vacation... 113
42. Celebrating the Christmas season 112
43. Minor infractions with the law 111

The more changes you have, the higher the risk of getting sick in the future:

Over 400 Change Units - 80% chance of sickness

250 to 399 Change Units - 50% chance of sickness

Under 250 Change Units - 30% chance of sickness

When a death destroys your future plans, wishes, dreams, dashes your hopes and push you to the brink of despair, it's important to take care of your health. When picking up the pieces of your shattered life, don't go without food and rest while working to bring new meaning back into your existence. It may take you years to find ways to ease your pain and take away the despair.

Death affects your attitude, temperament, level of tolerance, and lowers your self-confidence. It robs you of your stamina and undermines your emotional foundation. Death is like selective adaptation, if you want to survive, you must adapt to the many changes death demands.

CHAPTER 14

<u>Grief and Emotions</u>

When Marlene tried to accept her mother's death, she went through various stages of anger and despair. Many times she'd overstep, the boundaries in relationships when she turned them into something they weren't. If a relationship didn't work out to her satisfaction, she'd grieve all over again and blame others for her unhappiness.

Everything unpleasant that happened to Marlene was magnified ten times over. To cope with her sadness, Marlene pretended to be happy when she wasn't. She didn't handle her anger well, and was a bitch with anybody who said or did anything to her she didn't like. A lot of relationships were severed and never repaired during her period of grieving.

"Time" helped Marlene the most. It has taken all of ten years for her to put the loss of her mother into a healthy perspective and find closure.

In Frieda's situation, she felt her anger and grief were private, and didn't want anyone to get physically or emotionally close to her. She chose to resolve her own pain at her own pace through meditating, practicing self-hypnosis, listening to motivational tapes, and talking to the deceased. For her it worked.

Any memory that brings tears to your eyes needs to be remembered, even those coming out of despair and anger. Go over and over the emotional feelings you had with the deceased and re-live the relationship. Take a few minutes each day to talk to the deceased. Tell them how much you miss and love them, and how much you enjoyed having them in your life. Review the good times you shared.

Repetition will give you the strength necessary to withdraw your emotional energy from your loved one, and redirect it into a substitute. Reflecting allows you to disassociate from the pain and anguish death has brought, and release yourself from the emotional charge that once connected you to the deceased when he/she was alive.

Each time you talk about your relationship with your love one, you become tougher emotionally, and will strengthen your resilience.

CHAPTER 15

<u>Physical Well-Being</u>

You have no control over death. It's final, and you must deal with it. You can't change what has happened, so stop trying to undo the loss, and find ways to cope; otherwise, the psychological conflict will throw your body out-of-balance.

Losing an only brother is tough. Frank is still adjusting, and gets through each day with help from his friends and his little nephew, Tony. He and Tony are like brothers. Frank is working through the grieving process by exercising, lifting weights, jamming on his guitar, and playing basketball and football once a week with his friends.

Frank is still in mourning. He still thinks of his brother in the present and feels as though he is still alive. In his mind the only difference is that he can't physically touch, see, or hear him. Everyday when he goes to work, he passes the cemetery where his brother is resting. Everyday he waves to him. He has not let go.

During his brother's illness, he was there for him everyday. He hated seeing him fighting to live, and to cheer him up, they talked a lot about sports, current events, Tony, and ate pizza. Frank still feels empty, but Scott pleaded for him to be strong. Frank cries when he's alone and will always be sad, but won't admit it. His grieving is guarded, and personal.

When Scott was alive, Frank loved him and never tried to disrespect him. He gave him support to the end. He was the one with him when the end came. Frank has no guilt, only anger at the doctors who couldn't save him. All Frank has left are memories. For awhile he refused to eat and lost weight, but now, he's getting adequate rest and eats a balanced diet.

Mourning is not the time to worry about weight. The nervous system needs all the nutritional foods it can handle to take care of the continuing daily demands of living when grieving. Eating keeps the weight and resistance up, and avoids disturbing the homeostasis as the body scrambles to protect itself from invading germs. Food and rest protects the immune system, and keeps any biochemical reactions that might affect the heart rate at bay. Adequate rest, sleep, and exercise stimulates the digestive tract and keeps the metabolic rate normal.

When grieving, it's wise to stay away from drugs, alcohol, and sedatives. There are no quick fixes or short cuts from the pain grief generates. Establish a symbol, create a ritual, or join a support group to help you disconnect from the deceased and start building a new life. If you're a physical person with a high energy level, get involved in strenuous activities. Use exercise as a vehicle for grief relief.

Sex when grieving, means different things to different people. Mixing the two may precipitate more stress. If you want to indulge yourself in excessive copulation as an outlet for your grief relief, and your mate wants to refrain from sex, you need to compromise. If you can't, and tempers begin to flare, seek couples therapy or talk to your clergy. Trying to resolve grief, amidst marital fighting only prolongs the grieving process.

CHAPTER 16

<u>Social Adjustment</u>

It took awhile for Sherri to learn to handle her grief and deal with it one day at a time. Her husband, Scott, was diagnosed with a fatal illness and died two years later, but before he expired he looked beyond his death and talked to his wife about her life after he was gone. Those early talks gave Sherri the strength that paved the way for her to overcome her pain.

After Sherri's husband died, there was a great deal of denial. Whenever she felt sad, she'd stop and think about how blessed she was to have had him, if only for a little while, as a husband and friend. Sherri sat for hours looking at pictures and reflecting on the happy times they had during their ten years of marriage.

After looking at old photos and videos over and over, she came to realize how much she had to be thankful for. Then she'd give herself a pep talk, and go take a long walk. Sometime she'd exercise.

Sherri knew her loving husband didn't want her to sit around being sad. He wanted her to get out and live for the two of them.

Sherri's biggest fear was being abandoned and having to raise their son, Tony, alone. She buried her anger and feelings of abandonment, and covered her fears up by trying to be understanding. After all, she knew her husband didn't want to leave his family ... he had no control over his situation --- he didn't ask to be stricken with a fatal disease.

Sherri believed Scott's death was "God's will," but that belief did not resolve her anger. It displaced it and prolonged her grieving process by making her mean spirited.

It's terrifying when you lose a mate or a companion. You no longer have an ally to rely on and provide you with a sense of belonging. You feel there's no one to secure a place in this world for you, or give you a reason for being. You are permanently separated. You have nobody to talk to, exchange smiles with, share information, or engage in social activities.

Your emotional security is gone. Death has robbed you of a

social life. Whenever you are invited out by friends or family, or asked to dine and dance, you don't feel comfortable. You feel out-of-place because you have nobody to be close with, smooch with, or meet your emotional, physical, and social needs. You are alone and only half a person.

Sometimes when a mate dies, the surviving spouse's grief is reflected in urges to go on partying sprees, visit old dance places, fun vacation spots, frequent familiar restaurants, or just hang out at the cemetery.

Some find comfort going through their spouse's personal effects, dressing up in their clothes, putting on their jewelry, make-up or spraying themselves with perfumes and colognes. This is all part of grieving. Just remember that wearing the deceased's jewelry or clothing, looking at pictures or reading old love letters won't bring them back. Trying to recapture what you've lost may backfire, and make you feel worse because you've fueled your sense of loss which will generate more anger.

In the case of Jeremy, he drank himself into a stupor once a week after his mother died. He became anti-social and so combative, his father bought a gun for protection. Anger had Jeremy's personal space bubble so inflated, no family member or friend wanted to invade his bubble. They walked around him like he had the plague. He blamed his mother for all of his problems. He blamed her for helping the doctors kill her, and for leaving him.

Two years later, Jeremy's attitude was still bad, he was still angry, still in pain, and had done little to transfer the emotional energy he once had in his mother into something constructive. Jeremy refused to grieve. To him, it was a sign of weakness.

Grieving is hard, but you can make coping easier if you abide by the following and avoid the don'ts: Don't give-up, and don't allow grief to push you into the depths of despair. Don't turn into something you don't want to be, and watch out for the vices. Don't become a gambler or alcoholic, and don't do drugs. Don't get involved in criminal activities, and don't become sexually promiscuous. Take your time, and don't rush into a long-term relationship, and last, don't eat to cope.

Going through the grieving process makes you vulnerable.

Your thinking is flawed, and you should give yourself time to work through your grief and learn who you are. Get involved with counseling, clergy, or a support group to help you with your outlook. You are in the midst of modifying your behavior, and struggling to become more comfortable and confident with who you are.

Reach out to others. Let them help you help yourself. Look up old friends, join social clubs, go to church, seek new hobbies, and explore new pursuits.

CHAPTER 17

<u>Financial Grief</u>

Generally, the financial grief associated with death comes from deprivation, detachment, and a struggle to understand what has been lost, and what will be lost in the future, emotionally, and financially. If there is a shortage of money, you're going to start worrying about surviving. If you were comfortable living on two salaries, and ask, "how am I going to pay the mounting bills on one salary," you're facing a nightmare.

In a perfect world, financial matters would have been worked out in advance. The deceased would have preplanned his demise and made arrangements for the security of his family through insurance, savings, or financial planning. Wills would've been drawn up and reviewed. Special files would've been maintained for insurance benefits, pension plans, social security, and other investments, but since this is not a perfect world, you may be one of the families left in a needy position.

Years ago when women married and went from daddy's home into husband's house, most were kept financially illiterate because it was a "man thing" to handle the money. Back then, when ol' John upped and died, poor Sally didn't know how to pay a bill or write a check. In those days, when women were left in precarious positions, many didn't know how to care for themselves or their children. They became dependent on their families, well-meaning friends, their church, or some woman's husband. Widowed women were often ostracized and friendships terminated by their married friends because they couldn't trust their husbands to be gentlemen, and not confuse compassion and helplessness with love, and they couldn't trust their widowed friend to be a lady and respect the vows of the male friend assisting her.

People don't like to talk about death and dying, and as a result, more than seventy-five percent of surviving families are not prepared. Many times, not even a will has been drawn. The subject is taboo. However, if you are one of the many left without benefit of financial preplanning, follow the guideline outlined below: A. Make a list of names, phone numbers, and addresses of relatives, friends and business associates. B. Make a directory of people you need to contact by phone in the event of a death:

1. Funeral home personnel to advise of death
2. Cemetery to set up memorial services
3. The person giving the eulogy
4. Pall bearers
5. Preacher, priest, rabbi, etc.
6. Newspaper for the obituary
7. Office of vital statistic for death certificate
8. Inform employer of death
9. Your attorney regarding estate matters
10. Life insurance representative
11. Military pension organizations
12. Credit Unions
13. Fraternity affiliations
14. Social Security office
15. Medicare for forms to take care of any payment for services
16. Banks, savings and loans, or mortgage companies, regarding name change
17. Landlord, if renting
18. Offices of pension plans, mutual funds, stocks and bonds to obtain forms for benefits and name change
19. Financial consultant to make revisions
20. County Recorder regarding title changes
21. Post office, DMV, Pacific Bell, Dept. of Water and Power, garbage collection, department store accounts, credit card companies, clubs, cable television, charities, etc. for removal of the deceased's name.

Records that Should Be Locked Up

a. Wills and living trusts
b. Safe deposit container and key
c. Passbooks and bank accounts
d. Annunities, CD's and T-bills
e. Cash and mutual funds
f. 401K's, IRA's and Keogh accounts
g. Social security information
h. Veteran records
i. Insurance policies
j. Deeds and promissory notes
k. Stock market information
l. Personal and secured loans
m. Balances on loans
n. Business contracts
o. Partnership information
p. Real estate records
q. Vehicle records of ownership
r. Current and past income tax records
s. Credit cards, warranties, birth certificates, passports, contracts

Burial and memorial information should be tucked away in a safe place. Did the deceased want to be buried or cremated. Does the deceased want to donate any of his organs. What kind of service does he want.

Before Scott died, he sat down with his mother, Frieda, and told her where he wanted to be buried, how, and what type of service he wanted. He was money conscious and made it very clear that the family spend the minumum amount to put him away. Scott saw no need for pall bearers or escorts, and felt one limousine to carry the family to and from the cemetery was ample. He stipulated the type of music he wanted, and that his casket be closed. Scott was vain and wanted people to remember him when he was looking good.

Lack of money and lack of financial preplanning is a cruel legacy for a deceased to leave behind. It breeds anger, stress, and the kind of trauma that stands in the way of the grieving process.

Emily was devastated when her husband was killed. He left her with six children, no savings,and rent due. Her only recourse was welfare until his social security began. She was a high school drop out with no marketable skills. Out of the ten thousand dollar life insurance policy her husband had, a third of it went for burial expenses and to pay delinquent bills. The balance went to find a cheaper place to live.

Had Emily's husband planned just a little bit, she wouldn't have had to get into the grim task of counting dollars and sorting through legal documents immediately after the funeral. No grieving family deserves that type of legacy when caught in the clutches of grief.

Should death be swift as in an accident, suicide or murder, no one is ever prepared to deal with someone being here one day and gone the next. If death is slow, nursing care may become more difficult as the illness stretches into months and/or years, and require larger and larger investments of time, effort, energy, and financial planning.

Should you find yourself in that kind of long-term stressful situation, take care to avoid running the risk of getting sick. Watch how much emotional and physical energy you expend. Whatever financial difficulties the deceased may have created for you, function in the here and now. If your finances are limited, help is out there with friends, family, social services and community support groups. Go to the yellow pages and remember, nothing ever stays the same," Life goes on."

CHAPTER 18

<u>Displaced Grief</u>

Everybody handles their grief in a different way, and some grieve the dying of another by acting out as Xavier did when doctors told him his wife had ovarian cancer. The primitive thoughts laying dormant in his subconscious mind kicked-in. His fight/flight instinct took over, and he began walking around the hospital stealing paper clips, band aids, and hiding them in his pockets. The chemical changes taking place in Xavier's brain and body made him aggressive, combative, destructive, and anti-social. He became angry, and territorial. Stealing and hiding supplies represented the flight mechanism, and being combative with the staff was acting out his fight instinct. A psychiatrist placed him on a seventy-two hour hold, and when he settled down, and began to grieve, his flight instinct gave way to anxiety, and his fight instinct to depression.

When seventeen year old Frank's grandmother died, he "lost it". The day before she was buried, he walked into a department store, tried on a pair of under shorts and walked out. A store detective caught him, brought him back to security and called his mother, Frieda.

Frank had money in his pocket, but had an overwhelming need to lash out at someone or something. He was stressed, anxious, fearful, deprived, and didn't know where to constructively channel his anger. He was in mental turmoil.

CHAPTER 19

A Child's Grief

Resolving a child's grief is getting him/her through their fears of abandonment and insecurity by creating an environment of physical stability, and a climate of emotional security. Before Scott died, he helped his child by distancing himself so as to make his son's adjustment easier. Whenever he talked to Tony, he told him how much he loved him and that Uncle Frank, and Grandpa Mario, would be taking his place and caring for him when he's gone.

After Scott expired, Tony had fears about being abandoned and became clinging and touchy-feely. Hugging, kissing, rubbing, and sitting on laps gave him emotional security. Tony needed something real and tangible, something he could grasp and hold. Touching made people real, and assured him that who he was close to, was alive.

Stability in Tony's life was very important. He was not up rooted or moved around, and no significant changes were made in his living pattern. His grandparents did everything to make him feel secure. They fixed a bedroom for him in their house, and his Uncle and Aunt did the same thing. This gave him a sense of belonging and having something of his own.

In each room he had his own toys, clothes and miscellaneous belongings. This cemented his security. During the first year when he stayed over night with grandma and grandpa, he'd spend part of the night in bed with them.He needed their closeness. He needed emotional security. He needed to feel secure and confident they would not leave him.

Grandpa Mario and Uncle Frank are role models for Tony, and they give him the male attention, discipline, and love required to develop into a stable young man. Today, at age nine, Tony's a well adjusted boy. He makes friends easily at school, plays the piano with grandpa, and rides motorcycles with Uncle Frank. They play basketball, football, and Tony challenges both to video games. He rides bicycles with granny. She picks him up from school and helps him with his school assignments.

Tony remembers his dad and the times they spent together exploring nature. He remembers being taught to ride his tricycle and his dad reading to him. He still can't understand why his dad had to die. Tony is good company to his mother and he has become the little man of the house.

According to a chart on age related progress for children from childhood to adulthood, Tony's developmental skills were right on target from age six to eleven as follows:

I. Cognitive:

1. He's capable of using logic to put different things in order
2. He can tell time
3. Has begun to think and reason abstractly; can classify and handle situations; is able to test conditions
4. Pleased over school accomplishments
5. Likes to read
6. Has begun to see things from different angles
7. His attention span and thinking skills have increased
8. He operates in the present
9. He follows rules

II. Psychosocial

1. Peers, family, and teachers are the most important people in his life
2. Friends are more important than family
3. He pushes hard to be a success at what he does
4. He strives to belong and gain approval of peers
5. His behavior is controlled by anticipation and/or the expectation of praise or blame
6. He considers intention when judging behavior
7. Loss of control is a serious fear
8. He enjoys exploring the neighborhood
9. He enjoys using the phone
10. He enjoys playing games with rules

At the time of Scott's death, Sherri was grappling with her own demons and was almost out-of-control. It took her all of five years to work through her grief and be there emotionally for Tony. When she reached closure, she mellowed out and found peace with herself. She controlled her anger and brought her sadistic and masochist tendencies into balance.

CHAPTER 20

<u>Other Griefs</u>

Grief wears many hats, and we grieve the loss of something from the time we get up until we go to bed. The degree of grief lies in the importance of the loss. Most minor griefs are often taken for granted and fall in the category of annoyance or some slight irritability as follows: Fall and break something, bruise your arm, be late for work, burn your dinner, have an accident, etc.

Anything that angers you causes grief and should be grieved; otherwise, the tension will build up and display itself in a displaced fashion. Grief is a cover all for anything that represents a loss--death and dying just happens to be the most severe loss of all.

Whether your children are leaving home, you lose your job, have your money stolen, lose your health, etc., you need to grieve and let go. Letting go of anything ranges from a few seconds to a few years.

The weekend sport enthusiasts who batter their wives are exercising sadistic tendencies; otherwise, they wouldn't be hitting them. Many people think a night in the slammer for battery will cool hubby off, but it doesn't. Sitting in jail over night filled with rage only aggravates the situation, and guarantees the wife another beating. What the husband should do is come to grips with what he has done and try to resolve his anger. He needs to find the origin of his violence, destroy his bad attitude, and mourn it's loss the same way he would mourn the loss of a person. Instead he sits in jail stuck in the second stage of grief--anger.

It makes no sense to hit a spouse over a ball game because their team lost or because they missed a play the last ten seconds. Frank loves sports, and his dad taught him not to go overboard and allow a game to take all of his attention and consume his energy. A game is supposed to offer entertainment, not be used as an outlet for male aggression.

Watching games is fine, but it's the ball player who reaps all the benefits. He makes all the money, and gets all the exercise and glory. What does the observer get? If he's lucky, he gets to spend his money on an expensive ticket, get fat eating junk foods, and if he batters his wife, a trip to jail. It makes no sense.

Situation: Husband watching the Tyson fight...the boxer is losing ... the husband has $20 riding on the fight ... the match is down to the last few seconds. The wife comes in and says, "Is the match about over? I'm tired of waiting, dinner is getting cold."

Her statement distracts her husband. He misses the left jab and becomes livid. His adrenalin skyrockets. Already pissed, the interruption is the last straw. His sado-masochistic tendencies surge out of control, and he hits his wife without thinking. Releasing all of that bottled up aggression feels good, and he pops her again.

The boxing match is over, the husband has lost and needs to lash out. "Bam!" He hits her again. The wife breaks away and runs into the bedroom. She locks the door, and calls the police. Shortly, there's a knock at the door. The police comes in just as the wife runs out of the bedroom sporting a black eye and split lip. Hubby is carted off to jail.

Any unresolved grief, anger or trauma resulting from a death, divorce, or financial loss, will in time, come back to haunt you whenever you are stressed-out, uptight or "overloaded." When grief becomes displaced and you can't get past the anger trap, use the repetition process.

Go over whatever you have lost and are grieving about. Do so until the sting is gone and you can disconnect from whatever loss you're grieving over and move on with your life.

CHAPTER 21

<u>Depression</u>

Depression happens when your primitive fight/flight escape mechanism fails, and your conscious mind can no longer handle the repressed conflict. Your conscious mind becomes "overloaded" and shuts down and lets your subconscious mind take over. Depression is an escape mechanism. You're running from reality.

Depression makes you want to escape into a deep sleep. Your body is malfunctioning, your brain is in mental turmoil, and your self-regulatory parasympathetic nervous system is forced to come to your rescue. It protects you by reducing your fight/flight reaction to a slow passive rate. You lose your will to fight or take flight and you go into a sleep-like state. This is the best way to handle depression. Sleep enables you to vent. Sleep lets the subconscious mind get rid of your unresolved conflict.

If for some reason, sleeping doesn't remove the repressed guilt, and you awaken still feeling tired and anxious, you have a blockage. And to remove the blockage you need to act out. Find a pillow and scream and yell into it until you're hoarse. Cry, talk to friends, relatives, clergy, and if nobody is around, talk to yourself. It's imperative that you verbally express yourself anyway you can. If that doesn't remove the blockage, seek counseling to help you with your anger or guilt.

There are three types of dreams: The wishful thinking dreams takes place during the first part of the night. These dreams are about what took place in your life during the day. The second type of dreams are called precognative dreams. These take place during the middle of the night, and are predicting dreams. They are about the information you've gathered and accumulated through what you've heard, seen or experienced during your daily living.

The venting dreams are the third and final dreams that occur at the end of the night. These dreams are the most important because they clear your mind of the fears, doubts, traumas and events you don't need. Venting dreams are like computers, "garbage in-garbage out". These are the dreams which gets rid of what you don't need to hold on to.

Go to that safe place within your mind. If it's in the sun, get comfortable and relax. Close your eyes and visualize rays of warm beams shining down on you, and filling your mind and body with positive healing energy that dissolves and washes away all of the negative thoughts that have been holding you back in life. Feel the knowledge, wisdom, and understanding flowing into every cell of your body. Take a deep breath, hold it for ten seconds, then exhale. Your slow breathing brings relief from stress because the inner and outer levels of your mind are being cleansed.

Let your muscles go limp as you feel a soft tranquil sensation move from the tips of your toes to the top of your head. You feel like a rag doll, lax and loose. Your muscles tighten and tense up as you inhale, and relax and release tensions, fears, and anxieties when you exhale.

A. Mental ways to protect yourself from depression:

1. Keep a repertoire of positive tapes in your mind, and when a negative thought begins to replay, reject it and replace it with a positive tape. Build a library of positive tapes in your mind, and repeat the healing statements several times a day. Use visualization to build a protective shield around you to keep out all negative influences and forces. This shield will allow you to enjoy your life more fully because only the good will penetrate that shield.

B. Physical ways to fend off depression:

1. Laugh! Laughing is therapeutic. Train yourself to laugh. Sit before a mirror and role play. The ability to tell jokes and create humor creates a positive state of mind that helps you maintain an up beat level and keep depression at bay. Laughing is good for the soul, it gives you the wisdom to think and function in a more rational manner. You remember the happy events in your life and respond favorably, but if you're feeling sorry for yourself and sink into a low emotional state, your thoughts become biased and your reactions become negative.

2. Music speaks to the conscious and subconscious. It helps you discover your inner self and become positive. Music is a mental escape. It provokes day-dreaming, and allows you to drift into an imaginary world. Music bridges the gap between the real and unreal and helps you find yourself.

3. If everything else fails, chant. Singsong the following phrases until the negative feelings within you dissipate. I like myself... I like myself... I like myself... I love myself... I love myself... I love myself. I feel fantastic, I love myself and I like myself, etc.

CHAPTER 22

<u>Anger</u>

Dolly and Wilbur were active socialites always on the go until Wilbur became seriously ill and needed around-the-clock care. Adjusting to staying at home was almost too much for Dolly, and she began lashing out. She blamed Wilbur for ignoring his health, coming down sick, and abandoning her. She was ready to explode, but didn't want the hired help to know how angry she was. She would wait until the nurse left the house on a lunch break, then she'd go into Wilbur's room and give him hell.

In the beginning, anger was Dolly's biggest stumbling block. She couldn't get past her rage and wanted to physically hurt Wilbur. Her sadistic tendencies were reaching the breaking point, and she needed to find a way to dissipate her rage before she did something she'd regret. Frieda advised Dolly to take a picture of Wilbur, place it on a pillow, get a hammer and symbolically beat him until her anger was gone. The beating would be for inconveniencing her, humiliating her, not being there for her, and turning her into a half a person. Frieda further urged Dolly to talk to Wilbur's picture as she beat him. Yell at him, cuss him, and let him know how she feels. Let him know about the pain he has put her through. Frieda assured Dolly that when she finished working him over, she'd feel like a new person and her rage would subside.

Once Dolly got passed her anger and reached acceptance, she learned to turn off emotionally and tune Wilbur out physically. In doing so, Wilbur thought Dolly was insensitive, but she was worried about her health and had to be careful. She recently had had surgery. Who would care for her if she became stressed out.

Every night Dolly sought peace behind closed doors. She'd lock herself in her bedroom, close out the world, and grieve what she had lost. Dolly loved to read and after reading a good book, she'd meditate, pray, and listen to relaxing cassette tapes.

Seeking quiet time allowed her to recharge her emotions and continue searching for new meaning.

As soon as Dolly accepted that her husband would forever be an invalid, she rejoined her friends and returned to her art and bible study classes. Dolly began taking walks amidst nature and long drives to listen to jazz. She loved clothes and began shopping for materials to begin sewing again. She scheduled a trip a month with her senior citizen friends and did things to make her feel good about herself. Twice a month she humored herself by eating out.

Wilbur was angry and jealous when she'd go out and leave him, but Dolly felt no guilt, she was the best friend he had. She provided him with the best care money could buy, and around-the-clock companionship.

To keep whole, Dolly had to do something. She felt like a hostage in her own home and had to get out and make some kind of life for herself. She and Wilbur's lives were now separated, and Dolly had disconnected. She transferred her emotional energy once invested in Wilbur into other people, places, and things.

CHAPTER 23

<u>Displaced Anger</u>

It angered Frieda, watching her son, Scott, deteriorate before her eyes. Death offered her no choice, and having no choice generated rage. Frieda hated being forced to accept something she had no control over. She wanted to lash out like a screaming, kicking, yelling, out-of-control child, but society would frown on such actions, and put her in a psych ward.

Frieda felt she was a good person, and couldn't understand why this was happening to her. Granted people are born, live and die, but knowing that was not consoling to her. She was angry, depressed and wished she could close her eyes and never awaken, but she always did.

Every morning, she'd open her eyes, look around, cuss God, and ask Him what the hell did he have in store for her this day. Frieda no longer sprang out of bed anticipating good. She no longer viewed God as kind and merciful. She couldn't lash out at the doctors, they were doing the best they could. She couldn't blame medicine, it's a practicing art, and she couldn't blame science, they were trying. So, who was she to blame?

Frieda couldn't hold society responsible by holding up a bank or assaulting people, and she couldn't bury herself in sorrow or drink away her pain. Frieda needed a scapegoat, a focal point to place blame and vent anger, and God was it. Like a thief in the night, He came and stole her child, and she let Him have it.

Anger is a powerful emotion, and to help Frieda get through the grieving process, she took classes, piano lessons, wrote, exercised, listened to motivational tapes, and practiced deep relaxation.

There were times after Scott died that Mario would come unglued about his son being cut down in the prime of his life. He was a hardworking citizen contributing to society, and Mario had to be real careful when dealing with young men strung out on drugs or alcohol. Just looking at them infuriated Mario. His son was dead and these clowns are still alive serving no useful purpose.

It was a busy night at the clinic when a loud and obnoxious young man came in bragging about how good he felt taking drugs. Mario lost control. He threw the young man against the wall and for a split second he could've beat his brains out. An attendant intervened, and explained to the young man that Mario was grieving. He had recently lost his son who was a good kid. Knowing this calmed the young person down and before he left the clinic, he stopped by Mario's office to apologize for acting a jerk.

Mario still has moments of rage, but he deals with it by distancing himself from irritating people and going through the repetition process. Scott was special, and whenever Mario feels his spiritual presence he goes off and talks to him.

Scott has spoken to his dad only once, and that was the day after he was buried. Mario was under his car checking his brakes when a soft voice said, "Dad, don't worry about me, I'm fine." Getting this message so startled Mario he bumped his head sliding from underneath the car. He laid on the ground, and feeling relieved he cried.

Read the following affirmation, it will help you with your anger. Say it or write it until it becomes a part of your subconscious.

Everyday of my life, I live, I love and I'm happy. I exhibit peace and have tolerance toward others. People like me and I like them. I've come to realize that every personality is different. It's part of a person's heritage, and a sum total of their lifes' experiences. I realize that had I been born or raised in a similar environment, and survived a similar experience, I'd be just like that person and would probably act like him. Knowing that, I can accept others as they are. When people do things I disapprove of, that's a cue for me to do better, and a show of sympathy and understanding are the only emotions I feel and express. I can control me even when the situation is stressful. I enjoy a feeling of satisfaction and I pride myself for being able to focus and maintain control. Being in control allows me to express positive and healthy emotions that reflect love, caring, sympathy, and understanding toward others. When other people exhibit kind qualities, I love them for them. I forgive people because if I had the same body, thoughts, experience, and awareness, I'd be like them. Therefore, when people exhibit a bad attitude, I can forgive them because I understand and realize they are only expressing what I'd express if I were in their shoes. I am me, you are you and I respect your individuality. Everyday, I strive to have kind words, and a sincere smile for those I meet. I accept people for who they are and I know my pleasant attitude reaches out and touches them. I respect me and people admire my forgiving and soothing disposition. Treating others the way I want to be treated, makes me feel good about myself because love, understanding, and giving of one's self are the keys to happiness. By accentuating the positive emotions and eliminating the negative ones, helps me better understand those who are going through the pangs of anger and why. With a clear mind, I find it easy to choose the right words to keep me calm, serene and relaxed. I have the capacity to sympathize with people who have negative qualities, but can appreciate their good qualities. Being in control of my emotions improves my disposition and brings out the good qualities in me. I recycle my positive feelings back into my life every day, and I feel fantastic. My ability to be understanding is the foundation which allows me to look beyond a person's faults and forgive them for the bad things they've done to me. By thinking positive and rejecting the negative, I understand those who are angry and why. My subconscious mind absorbs all the good in my environment and feeds positiveness into my psyche. These emotions guide me. When I have a clear mind, I find it easy to remain calm, serene and focused. At all times, I'm in control of my emotions. I radiate good, positive feelings and push the negative ones away. As I experience personal growth with each passing day, I love myself more. I like people more, and I feel fantastic.

CHAPTER 24

<u>Guilt</u>

Ken and Emma were arguing. Ken was unemployed, couldn't find a job, and was distraught and depressed. Rent was due. Emma was angry, insensitive, and didn't take Ken serious when he said he was going to kill himself. Thinking he was kidding, Emma poo-pooed the threat, and left the room to look after their six month old baby. Thirty seconds later, Emma's world crumbled when a shot rang out. She rushed back into the room, and saw Ken laying on the floor with blood gushing from his wound. Emma freaked. Her screams brought neighbors, and someone called 911. Seeing Ken die became buried in her memory.

Ken's family blamed Emma for his death, and she blamed herself. She should've responded when Ken cried out for help, but at the time, anger was clouding her thinking. Now, she's using alcohol to dull her pain and wash away her guilt, but it isn't working. Guilt is the last link she has connecting her to Ken.

When guilt reaches deep into the psyche, it becomes the most difficult emotion to get rid of. It's what people fail to do, or should've done when the person was living expires. Guilt is about high expectations and standards that may become so unrealistic, nobody can live up to them, not even you. Then there is the "shame guilt", that haunts you when you're glad it was the deceased who died, and not you.

Regardless of how good you feel about the deceased, what he was or wasn't, or how often he or she got on your nerves or irritated you, a tinge of guilt is a normal reaction. Nobody's perfect, and you should try to forgive yourself, and find constructive ways to resolve your guilt. If high expectations are at the root of your problem, work to change your attitude about what you did or didn't do by doing something worthwhile, either for yourself or someone else.

The best way to reduce or overcome guilt is to reach inside

yourself and work with your subconscious mind. It serves as a memory bank that controls the activities you call habits. These learned behaviors are expressions of energy that you direct. Everything you have ever seen, heard, smelled, tasted, felt, or experienced is permanently stored in your brain, and self-hypnosis is the quickest way to reach your subconscious.

If religions teach forgiveness, and if God can forgive you, why can't you forgive you. If you must hate, hate what made you do what you did, and don't repeat it. Use positive suggestions to change your attitude, and conquer this guilt. The first step Mario took to reduce his guilt was to face his true feelings of self-hatred and anger. The next thing he did was to look inside himself. Through self-hypnosis, he accomplished the third step, which allowed him to begin working to modify his thinking. On a daily basis, he fed positive and forgiving affirmations into his subconscious.

Carrying around feelings of guilt serves no useful purpose. Stop making negative statements, i.e., "if I had done this that wouldn't have happened." That's naive. Self-punishment goes against the laws of nature. Nobody's perfect. Everyone makes mistakes, some are just worst than others. Even though your body belongs to you, you have no right to make it sick by punishing it with guilt.

Use the following affirmation to help you handle feelings of guilt. Find a quiet serene place. Relax, close your eyes or fix them on an object. Treat the affirmation like a prayer and say it when meditating. If you write it, write it seven times.

> Because I will maintain a healthy body and mind, I will forgive myself for all the past mean-spirited acts I have committed. By forgiving me, I've been able to remove the burdensome load weighing me down. By forgiving myself, I can forgive all the people I may have hurt. Since we're all part of an inherited gene pool and environmental surroundings, I want to enjoy the best that life can give us all. I enjoy contentment. I enjoy happiness. I enjoy

tranquility and I enjoy peace. When I forgive, I radiate goodness and love. Turning over a new leaf makes me feel worthwhile and free. I enjoy the feeling of satisfaction when knowing I can forgive and like myself. My entire body lights up when I feel good about myself and reach out to others.By respecting me and loving me, I'm able to respect and love others. I am a caring person. I am a giving person. Forgiveness has set me free. I radiate like a beacon showing others how powerful forgiveness is. It sets me free, and places me at peace with my world.

Here is another way to make restitution and resolve feelings of guilt. If the guilt is mild, donate to a worthy cause. Get involved. Give some time to a charity, write letters for the sick and shut-ins, send flowers to someone special, or take a group of children to McDonald's for lunch. Giving makes you feel good about yourself. You learn to value who you are and like yourself.

If you drink, stop! If you smoke, quit! Build your self-worth on a solid foundation. But if you find giving something back to society doesn't make you feel fantastic and remove much of your guilt, talk to your clergy or seek counseling.

CHAPTER 25

Suicide

People do a lot of bazaar things when they are loaded down with unresolved grief and anger. Suicide is hatched when emotional pain creeps into all areas of a person's life. Self-destruction is not to escape living it's to escape the pain and turmoil living has created. Suicide is an escape mechanism and to avoid it, people need alternatives. They need to be able to day dream, fantasize and hallucinate. They need to create constructive outlets for their pain.

The severity of suicidal thoughts depends on the degree of sadist and masochistic traits inherent in peoples' make up. If the scale tips toward masochism, the person feels self-death is their only out. He doesn't feel accepted. He's lonely and paranoid. He feels he's a failure and just wants to end it all. Most of the time, this person is so despondent, he can find no purpose in going on or in anything he has done. He feels totally helpless, and taking the next breath becomes an effort.

When a person reaches such depth of despondency and is intent on self-destruction, he will usually by-pass the stages of self-death because his thinking is irrational. Anyone who commits suicide doesn't have organized thoughts. If he did, he wouldn't kill himself. He'd find a way to get out of the quagmire he's in and live.

It was reported in the newspaper that a policeman in Oklahoma was a hero. He killed himself. Sometime after that terrible bombing, he slashed his wrist, got out of his car, walked a few feet, pulled out his gun and blew himself away. It's believed he was overwhelmed from seeing so much death, and couldn't handle the guilt associated with grief. He was going through a divorce, and having problems seeing his children was the last straw.

This man undoubtedly had feelings of helplessness. He was so despondent, all he wanted was out, and took steps to be sure he was dead and couldn't be brought back. Now tell me, was his thinking rational? No! His thoughts were not organized. Had they been, he wouldn't have done what he did. Thinking you're a failure is difficult to deal with, and that alone can destroy you.

The worst thing a person can do to his spouse, children and himself is self-destruct. That's sending one ugly message to the partner. In Doctor Oliver's situation, he hung himself. He weighed 240 pounds, and oh, man! Did that wipe his wife out? You betcha.

Mario worked with Doctor Oliver.

He knew he was having problems with his wife, and his suicide devastated her. She wanted everything, and tried to buy everything--a big house, Mercedes, position, but the good doctor couldn't keep up with all of her wants. Sometimes, he could hardly tend to his patients arguing with his wife over the phone. She always wanted to buy something, and he always told her they didn't have the money. Her favorite response was, "I don't care, you're a doctor."

Whenever Doctor Oliver refused to talk to his wife over the phone, she'd come to the clinic and cuss him out in front of the staff. This was most embarrassing to the doctor.

When word reached the clinic that he had killed himself, his colleagues were upset, but nothing compared to his wife. All the money was cut off, and there would be no more. The doctor, loaded down with debt, had shifted his burden to his wife. The hospital helped the doctor's wife financially get on her feet and then she was left on her own. Insurance companies do not pay off in the event of a suicide.

Deva was one of those simple broads who had no education beyond high school. She was a sweet little girl who thought she had the world by the balls--always donating big money to the church vying for recognition. She belonged to several committees, but when she had no money and could no longer participate in the many activities, she was angry, humiliated and hurt. Doctor Oliver did a number on her.

Then there was Doctor Edwards, who took a swan dive off the building. If Mario had been a few minutes later getting to work, Doctor Edwards would've landed on the steps in front of him. This man was a frustrated gay. He had a lovely wife and daughter, but had reached a point whereby he couldn't reconcile being straight any longer. He wanted to be gay, but had to maintain being straight when he didn't wanna be.

One minute, Doctor Edwards was in the clinic seeing patients, and the next minute he was gone. He walked out saying, "I'll be back," and the next thing anybody knew, word circulated that he had jumped off the building. In a spur of the moment, Doctor Edwards went upstairs and jumped off the building just like that. Nobody noticed he was gone until he was seen splattered on the ground.

Nobody knew how troubled the doctor was. Mario was the only one with a clue. He had observed Doctor Edwards' increasing reckless disregard for his profession. His masochistic and sadistic tendencies were unbalanced, and he had developed a "care less" attitude, and a blatant disregard for policy and procedure.

Doctor Edwards was head strung. Nobody could tell him anything. As his personality changed, he appeared to be on a collision course. Mario counseled Dr. Edwards several times, but he was going through that omnipotent invincible phase, and nothing Mario said made a difference.

Suicide is a complex subject even now, and psychologists, psychiatrists, doctors and nurses are still trying to figure out what to do about suicide.

People are put on seventy-two hour holds daily because they appear to be a danger to themselves and others, but when they're let out, doctors hope they're okay, but they don't know. All professionals know is that most people who have been institutionalized at sometime in their lives have suffered something traumatic at an earlier time in their lives.

CHAPTER 26

Reaching Closure

A. Checklist:

1. Identify what emotions you need to grieve, and
   start by asking yourself:
   a. Am I angry because I feel abandoned?
   b. Do I feel hopelessness because I cannot bring my love
      one back?
   c. Am I anxious because I am now alone?
   d. Does my frustration stem from not having enough
      money?
2. Go over the happy and sad times in your relationship.
3. Remenber each event, relive what happened, and review the
   reasons it happened.
4. Talk about the deceased. Talk about your hopes and dreams.
   Talk about the fantasies that bonded your relationship.
   Explore the ups and downs, causes and effects, crises and
   joys.
5. Act out your emotions and feelings by:
   a) Talking about your rage, guilt, and frustrations.
   b) Running, boxing a punching bag or beating the bed with
      your fists.
   c) Writing about your feelings. Learning to paint, draw,
      dance, or play the piano, etc.
   d) Exercising, swearing, screaming all release tension.
6. Doing strange things does not mean you are out-of-control.
   It just means you have a lot of emotions that you cannot
   handle by simply crying.
7. It's o.k. to express your anger by being bitchy. It's a normal
   reactions when grieving.
8. Don't compare yourself to others. This is your loss, your
   grief, and you can handle it anyway you like.
9. Work to resolve any hostilities and resentments against
   others, yourself, and God by getting involved. Join support

groups, social clubs, or talk to your clergy.

10. Don't shut down. Keep the tears flowing when talking and reviewing your relationship with the deceased.
11. Keep busy.
12. Escape your pain through sleep.
13. Time is your best ally.
14. Avoid taking tranquilizers to suppress your anger or guilt. They only delay the grieving process.
15. Despite the pain, handle the unfinished business. Make the necessary decisions affecting your life. If there is too much pain, seek assistance.
16. Grieve your secondary losses, one at a time using the repetition process.
17. Listen to subliminal tapes on anger control, depression, building self-esteem, and self-confidence.

Meditate and continue to feed positive affirmations into your psyche until you're strong enough to face the world. Each morning before you get out of bed, listen for thirty minutes to a tape. Allow your subconscious mind to absorb the positive messages and act on them.

Create new projects that will help you let go of the compassion you feel for the deceased and let you remember the joyful moments you shared.

People don't grieve the pleasant memories, they grieve the unpleasant ones. As you reach a plateau of acceptance, it will be the pleasant moments and cherished memories that you will remember. And until you've grieved to that point, there will be flashbacks of unresolved emotions.

CHAPTER 27

<u>Closure</u>

Closure comes when you've reviewed and examined all of your feelings and emotions again and again and feel resigned as you let each one go. Closure is when you can express a feeling and it no longer ties you to the deceased. Closure is when you can exhibit an emotion and the pain hurts a little less. Closure is withdrawing a little more of your emotional investment each time you remember the deceased.

You will know when you've reached closure. You will know when you've arrived at a level of acceptance, you will be able to maintain a comfortable distance from the pain, hurt, and anger death inflicted. You will have gone through a metamorphosis that will have prepared you to disconnect and let go of the emotional bond that once kept you connected to the deceased when he or she was alive.

When you have reached closure, you will be ready to put meaning back into your life, fill that empty void and move on. That's what your loved one would want.

The following affirmation will encourage you:

Every morning when I get out of bed, I experience an inner feeling of joy. The hurt which was a part of my grieving process has become more and more distant. I am being filled with inner energy that creates a joy in me. I have overcome a very painful ordeal and I feel good about myself. I feel good about succeeding. I feel good about my life, because I can now go on. I feel refreshed, alive, loved, and relaxed. I'm wide awake and the feeling of depression has turned into a feeling of high self-esteem and confidence. I want to jump and shout. During the day, as I overcome my grief, I can feel it translating into vibrant energy. I feel all the things I put on the burner, I can now tackle. I feel confident, wonderful, strong, calm, healthy and alert. I am at peace knowing that life goes on after a long period of grief and depression. I can now enjoy my life more and more as I conquer change and mature. I can see clearly the beauty around me, where as before I saw only darkness.

Nobody's promised a rose garden, and nobody know better than Frieda. Ten years before Scott expired, they were discussing self-dying and Frieda's concerns about getting old. Scott flashed a wide grin and said, "Mom, don't worry about getting old, I'll take care of you."

End

Bibliography

Ad HOC Committee: Nursing Education Council - Guidelines for Age Related Categories, Olive View UCLA Medical Center, 1996

Bender: David L. and Leone: Bruno - Death and Dying, Opposing View Points, Greenhaven Press, Minn.,1980

Burgen: Larry A. and William C. - Death and Dying, Theory/Research/Practice, Wm. C. Brown Publishing Company, Iowa, 1979

Donnelly: Katherine F. - Recovering From The Loss of A Child, Macmillan Publishing Co., 1982

Fromm: Eric - Escape from Freedom, Holt, Rinehart and Winston, 1968

Fromm: Eric - For The Love of Life, Division of Macmillan, Inc., New York, 1986

Hammond, D. Corydon - Handbook of Hypnotic Suggestions and Metaphor, W.W. Norton & Company, N.Y. 1990

Holmes, Thomas H. - The Social Readjustment Rating Scale Journal of Psychosomatic Research, 11.213-218, 1967

Kappas, John G. - Professional Hypnotism Manual, Panorama Publishing Company, 3rd edition, 1987, Panorama, CA

Kubler-Ross: Elisabeth - On Death and Dying, MacMillan Publishing Co., N. Y., 1969

O'Connor: Nancy - Letting Go With Love: The Grieving Process, La Mariposa Press, 1984

Parkes: Colin Murray: Bereavement Studies of Grief in Adult Life, International University Press, N.Y., 1972

Petterle: Elmo A. - Getting Your Affairs In Order Shelter Publications, Bolinas, CA., 1993

Rando: Theresa A. - Grieving, How to Go on Living When Someone You Love Dies, Lexington Books, D.C., Heath Co., Lexington, Mass. 1988

Tebbetts: Charles: Self-Hypnosis and Other Mind-ExpandingTechniques, Westwood Publishing Company, Glendale, CA.,1987

About the Author

Katherine Jones has a BA degree in journalism from California State University at Northridge. She is a retired secretary, and resides in the San Fernando valley with her husband, son and two grandchildren.